THE SURPRISING YEARS

Understanding Your Changing Adolescent

A Book for Parents

Developed by

Lions Clubs International

and

Quest International

This edition of *The Surprising Years: Understanding Your Changing Adolescent* is part of the revised, expanded version of the *Skills for Adolescence* program. The book is essentially the same as earlier editions except for minor changes. These include new illustrations, new photographs, and other adaptations that make the book appropriate for use in both Canada and the United States. Examples are the inclusion of metric measurements and the deletion of such phrases as "our country."

Quest International
537 Jones Road
P.O. Box 566
Granville, Ohio 43023–0566
614/587–2800

Because of their longstanding commitment to young people and families, the following organizations have joined with Quest International and Lions Clubs International to bring you this book.

American Association of School Administrators

National Council of Juvenile
and Family Court Judges

National Federation of Parents for
Drug-Free Youth

National Middle School Association

National PTA

Pacific Institute for Research and Evaluation

CONTENTS

PART FIVE: ALCOHOL AND OTHER DRUGS— SOME QUESTIONS AND ANSWERS

SETTING THE STAGE

You bought him new jeans three months ago, and they're already too short.

You take the family to the movies, and she sits four rows in front of you.

You call home, he answers the phone, and you mistake him for his younger sister.

You call home, he answers the phone, and you mistake him for his older brother.

You suddenly realize one day that your daughter has become so mature and intelligent that she's almost not a child any more.

You told him you'd take him to the hockey game Thursday night, but when you get home from work, you're too tired to go. He slams the door, locks it, and stays in his room, sulking, the rest of the evening.

She spends an hour in the bathroom staring at the mirror.

When you were feeling sad recently, your son gave you a hug and told you he loved you. You were so proud of him.

You're Not Alone

Whoops! Check the birth certificate. It sounds as if you have a young adolescent on your hands—fancy words for children between the ages of 10 and 14. But don't panic. Millions of people make it through this time of life year after year. In fact, every adult in the world once lived through it.

It can be a trying period for you and your child, but it can also be a period of great joy and discovery.

In a way, "child" isn't such a good word for kids this age. Your youngster is starting to be almost a grown-up. That's one of the rewards of early adolescence for both of you. Adolescence isn't something to be afraid of. It can be a truly enjoyable period for you and your child. It's a time when kids really begin to come into their own.

This book shares some observations about the joys of the early adolescent years—and the struggles. If you are having problems, it offers positive suggestions that can help to make things better for your whole family.

The Typical Young Adolescent?

One of the most important questions young adolescents ask themselves over and over again is "Am I normal?"

Given the surprises and changes of this time of life, you may be asking the same question about your child. Why did he do that? Why did she say that? What did that mean? What really is normal?

During your years as the parent of a young adolescent you're going to discover a lot of things. Many of these will be mentioned in this book. If you have older teenagers, you may already be aware of some of the issues. Either way, you are in a unique position to help your child, and this book can help you understand your child even better than you do already. It can help you feel more comfortable and confident during these sometimes puzzling and challenging years. The book will give you a clear idea of what is normal and what isn't, when you should back off and when you might need to take some kind of action.

The Purpose of This Book

One purpose of the book is to explain the different changes of adolescence. Your child may be experiencing some of these right at this moment. Other changes may still be a couple of years away, but most of them will occur at some point. The important thing is for you and your child to be prepared.

Another purpose of the book is to give you a clear picture of what it's like to be a young adolescent and how you as a parent can help to make these years better and happier for everyone involved.

Many adults have somehow lost track of their own early teen years. Now that your child is going through this possibly difficult period, he or she needs someone who understands. This book is one way of reminding you about aspects of early adolescence that have always been true, as well as other things that are part of today's new generation.

For example, a 14-year-old girl in a large suburban town ran away from home recently after a family argument. She only went down the street to a friend's house, and she was gone only two hours. Nevertheless, her parents were devastated. They were so embarrassed that they never told anybody. Later they discovered that almost 30 percent of today's young people run away from home at least once during early adolescence (1). They wished they'd known that when their daughter did it. This doesn't mean that running away is okay—runaways often get into serious trouble. If the parents had known how common it is for teenagers to run away, however, they might not have felt so completely alone.

This book will help you know and understand such things.

The book also offers suggestions for building a good relationship with your child. You may find yourself saying, "Well, we already have a good relationship." If so, at least you'll know that someone else agrees with the approach you're using.

A Guide—Not a Book of Recipes

Whatever you think of the suggestions in this book, they're worth considering. All of them are based on sound research and on the experience of other parents. They have worked for real people in real-life situations. Because they've worked for others, there is a good chance they will work for you.

This book is not a "how to" manual. Its purpose isn't to tell you exactly what you should do as a parent—that has to be your own decision and will depend to a great extent on your values and your basic approach to raising children.

Think of it more as a guide to the territory, an overview of some of the most important issues. The "how to" will depend on how you view your role as a parent and how things are done in your family. It may also depend, to some extent, on your family's traditional ways of doing things and raising children. Some methods that worked for your own parents and even your grandparents may work for you.

For some families, of course, the early adolescent years are relatively free of problems. Early adolescence can be an exciting period of growth and discovery for everyone involved. This book is for these families as well as for families who may find the beginning of adolescence a somewhat bumpier time of life.

Drugs and Alcohol

An especially important part of the book is its goal of helping parents prepare their children to deal with the influence of alcohol and other drugs. Chances are that you have already given this matter some thought. Most parents today—and a great many adolescents too—are genuinely worried about the threat of alcohol and other drugs. Alcohol and drugs seem to be everywhere, and the stories of children and families being hurt by them are familiar to all of us.

Parents can play a vital role in protecting their children from alcohol and drugs—by learning all they can about the subject, by talking openly with their young teenagers, and by helping their children to grow up healthy and strong. This book contains many specific suggestions about how parents can help.

Boys and Girls Together

You will notice as you read this book that the examples used to make various points tend to focus either on a boy or a girl. Sometimes the book refers to "he or she."

It might be convenient if boys and girls in early adolescence were exactly alike. In fact, the differences between boys and girls this age are often dramatic. Girls tend to mature earlier than boys and have very different attitudes toward school, work, and a variety of other things in their lives (2).

Nevertheless, boys and girls also have many qualities in common during early adolescence. In order to make the book relevant to parents of both boys and girls, as much as possible the examples focus on ideas that are true for either sex. The best thing to do is read the entire book. Chances are you'll discover that most of the examples are relevant.

How the Book Is Organized

The book is divided into five parts:

- **Part One** is designed to help you understand something about the changes of the early adolescent years.

- **Part Two** deals with the all-important topic of building self-confidence in your child.

- **Part Three** focuses on communication between parents and young adolescents.

- **Part Four** talks about the importance of the family, with a special emphasis on discipline.

- **Part Five** addresses the issue of youthful drug and alcohol use—and how to prevent it.

Each section begins with a typical situation faced by young adolescents and their parents. Then there is a brief explanation ("A Closer Look"). Finally, each section concludes with "Some Thoughts," often in the form of practical tips about things you can do.

The book was designed to give you information and suggestions. It's not a set of rules that parents should follow. However, there are a few key things to remember in dealing with a young adolescent: don't forget that this person who is rapidly becoming an adult is still, in many ways, a child. Don't forget that this child-adult still needs you; hang in there and keep caring, even in moments when the going gets rough.

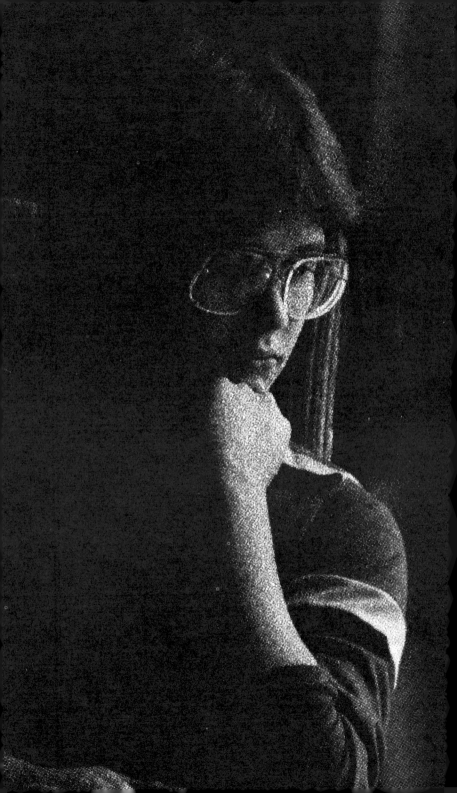

Part 1

The Changes of Growing Up

1

PHYSICAL GROWTH

Size vs. Maturity

Your son tries out for the junior high basketball team. Players come in all sizes. The coach is always joking around with the taller boys but doesn't seem to have time for the smaller ones.

A Closer Look

The years between 10 and 14 are a time of dramatic change. Perhaps the most obvious examples are changes in physical growth. Growth, or the lack of it, is easy to see, and the problems of growth are often obvious too.

Usually when young people enter adolescence they're rather childlike in size and features. By the time they're well into adolescence and no longer in the "early" phase, they look more like adults.

Most of the time this growth comes in a spurt. It seems to happen overnight. The adolescent growth spurt tends to begin about two years earlier for girls than for boys. Among girls the growth spurt generally peaks around the age of 12, and among boys it peaks around the age of 14. For both boys and girls, however, there is tremendous variation in when the growth spurt starts and how fast it progresses. That's why you might be surprised to see what look like "boys" and "men" playing together on a junior high basketball team.

The first day of school after the summer is always an exciting time both for students and teachers. Everyone stands around the halls and marvels at how much everyone else changed during the summer.

Growth spurts can create problems, however. For most of us looking at the young adolescent, physical growth is a mark of maturity. This is what the coach sees when he favors the taller boys. Similarly, if a 13-year-old boy is tall and already has some facial hair and muscles, we probably think that he's a rather mature young man capable of mature and responsible behavior. On the other hand, if a 13-year-old is short and frail, we tend to think we can't expect much maturity from him. In reality, the only difference between the two may be a simple matter of a three-month growth spurt. The smaller boy may actually be more mature in many ways—more disciplined, more capable, and more responsible than the larger boy. But most of us wouldn't have the same expectations of the two teenagers. We would be deceived by appearances.

Some Thoughts

Even if a 13-year-old is beginning to look like an adult, he or she is still just 13 years old. It may be easy to forget sometimes that your child is still a child, but you have the benefit of an adult point of view. That perspective can help you understand your child better. You may realize that he or she will eventually catch up with his or her peers, but for your child, a late growth spurt—or even a very early one—can be a difficult and embarrassing experience.

Clumsiness

Your tall, willowy 12-year-old daughter looks graceful when she's practicing modern dance moves, but at other times she has a way of bumping into things and appearing to be all arms and legs.

A Closer Look

Since your daughter is only 12, it's safe to assume that she hasn't had her new height to carry around very long. In fact, she probably grew quite a bit last summer. It's probably a real problem keeping her in clothes, particularly if she's the kind of kid who's always thinking about the way she looks.

Aside from the clothes problem, the height and weight can be difficult to deal with just on a physical basis. It takes time for a person to learn how to handle all that extra size. While she's learning to manage, she's going to be a little clumsy and awkward. The old-fashioned adjective for this is "gangly."

That physical clumsiness can lead to some other problems. For one thing, it's so obvious. People can generally cover up feeling somewhat insecure, but everybody can see gangliness. It's right out there, as plain as it can be. It's bound to cause a little embarrassment and self-consciousness, which will often make the suddenly large adolescent a little clumsy in social settings too.

Some Thoughts

Clumsiness hits personalities as well as bodies. You can help your child by explaining why sudden changes happen to so many young adolescents and emphasizing that they're normal.

2

OTHER BODY CHANGES

Girls and Boys

Now that your daughter is a young adolescent, she seems to be more interested in boys than anything else.

A Closer Look

Isn't growing up wonderful? You know her body is changing. You can look at her and tell that. She's taller and rounder and even fuller. But some other things are happening to her too, and we parents really fool ourselves if we try to ignore those other changes.

Your daughter is right in the middle of developing all the human reproductive capabilities—and normal feelings of sexuality too.

This process is called puberty. It happens when the body begins to create large amounts of the chemicals knowns as hormones, which send signals to the body that it's time for sexual growth to begin. People who live with young teenagers may get the idea that this period lasts forever. Actually, when you put puberty into the picture of an entire lifetime, a lot happens in a few short months. The changes of puberty can be as abrupt and surprising for your child as they are for you. Some young people really need help along the way.

In the last two years your daughter may have begun her monthly period. The majority of girls begin between the ages of 12 and 14, some as young as ten. That in itself can be a bit of a shock, and every girl needs help with it. A girl has to know what's happening to her body during puberty—and why. Even when girls have all the information they need, the beginning of the monthly period may cause some moments of fear, anxiety, worry, and embarrassment, particularly if the boys around them don't understand what they're experiencing.

Probably your 13-year-old has noticed that she has begun to look more like a woman. In our society one of the chief characteristics of womanhood is the development of breasts. If your daughter is like most girls, she views her breast development as a sign of her total maturity. If her breasts are growing, she may feel that she's mature and sophisticated. But if her breasts are small and underdeveloped, she may get impatient with the whole process.

Girls in early adolescence also begin to feel some rather adult sexual urges. It could be argued that these feelings are stronger and more extreme at this age than at any other. The newness creates curiosity and a variety of other emotions.

Your daughter is discovering some new feelings, and she's beginning to be aware that the world out there is full of boys. There is really nothing unusual about her, and probably there's nothing to be concerned about. But now is the time to provide her with some solid information about her body and about the role of sexuality in human relationships.

Some Thoughts

Puberty is one of the most important stages in a child's development. You can help your child to cope successfully with the changes of puberty by explaining what is happening and communicating that you know and understand. If possible, start to talk about puberty even before it happens. It shouldn't come as a surprise.

Boys and Girls

You overhear your son on the phone talking with a friend. The subject is sex—half joking, half serious—and you're shocked to hear how misinformed he is on some matters.

A Closer Look

Surprise! Kids this age are going to need some information about sex. They're enormously curious about it. That's absolutely normal. He has some questions, and he's going to get some answers, one way or another.

Ideally, he could get those answers from a reliable source such as a course in school—or, better yet, from you. But if he doesn't get them from a reliable source, he's going to get them somewhere else—from his friends, from movies, from magazines, from books, or through his own experimentation.

If you don't approve of any of those options, you need to take charge of instructing your child about his (or her) sexuality. Although you may get some help from a course offered by your child's school, this is too important a subject for you to leave to chance. At least check to make sure there is such a course.

In discussing sexuality with your child remember a few rules:

- Pick the right time, preferably when you're both feeling good about each other. Once probably won't be enough. You may need to have several talks about this important subject.

- Keep the lesson simple and honest. If you don't know the answer, admit it.

- Be clear about your values. Make sure your child understands how you feel about the role of sexuality in human relationships.

- It's okay to feel awkward talking with your child about sex. Most parents do. Be honest and do the best you can.

- Recognize that young adolescents may want and need to discuss their feelings about sexuality, not just "the facts." Often their feelings may be confused or unclear.

16

You can help by being a "sounding board" for your child's feelings and listening without judging or teaching. At the same time, this can be a chance to offer some low-key guidance.

Some Thoughts

Children are going to learn about sexuality from somewhere. Parents need to be part of their children's education in this area. Just as important as any specific information about sex, however, are your values regarding sexual relationships. You don't have to be a biology expert to tell your child what you believe.

3

CHANGES IN SCHOOL

Different Kinds of Schools

ACME NEW SCHOOL

A Closer Look

While we're expecting the young adolescent to adjust to body, mood, and personality changes, we also ask him or her to make some important educational changes. In fact, the transition from elementary school into junior high school is probably the most dramatic change a student will encounter during his or her school years.

Educators who have been concerned about the special needs of this age group have tried to make that transition a little easier. In the U.S., this has led to the creation of the middle school, a new approach to grade grouping. Traditionally junior high schools included grades 7 and 8, and maybe grade 9, in the same building. The middle school, on the other hand, is more likely to group together grades 6-8.

Whether your child's school is a junior high school or a middle school, it may also have some special programs designed to help young adolescents adjust to the new educational demands they're facing:

- Some schools have begun to offer a wider variety of courses so the student at this age can sample various areas of interest.

- Some emphasize teacher training in special skills for teaching young adolescents.

- Some offer a wide range of techniques like team teaching, core curricula (English and social studies taught together, for example), shorter classes, extended classes, and other unusual arrangements.

All of these are relatively recent experiments at designing an educational program to meet the specific needs of the young adolescent age group.

Some Thoughts

Since young adolescents have special needs and characteristics, schools for them need to be special too. Find out as much as you can about your child's new school. You may discover that you can help your child master the new school environment just by providing him or her with some information.

School Can Be Confusing!

Your 11-year-old daughter can't remember the name of her English teacher.

A Closer Look

This can happen easily to a child who has just made the transition from elementary school to junior high or middle school. Throughout her school life, up until grade 6 or 7, your daughter probably had only one teacher all year. That one teacher taught everything—math, science, reading, social studies, and English. Although your daughter might have been sent to another teacher a couple of times a week for P.E. or music, she still had basically one teacher who was very much like a parent.

Since she had only one teacher, she knew that teacher, and she knew she belonged to that teacher. Regardless of where she went around school or even around the neighborhood, she was in Mrs. Brown's class. That meant something.

But now that she's in junior high school, chances are that, like many other students, she's in the kind of school where the students change classes every 50 minutes or so. In other words, she has a different teacher and probably a different set of classmates for every period in the school day.

Not only has she lost that sense of being in Mrs. Brown's class, but now she has to learn the names of six or eight different teachers—and how to get along with them. That's a big adjustment to make.

You can help her. Since she no longer belongs to a special group at school, make sure she knows there is a group she belongs to somewhere. It might be just your own family. Or you might encourage her to get involved with activities like Scouts, 4-H, sports, or band that can offer her a sense of belonging.

Talk to her about all those different teachers. Try to get acquainted with her teachers yourself. Even if you have to take time off from work to go to open houses or teacher conferences, go. Your knowing your daughter's teachers will help her remember them—and maybe even what they're teaching her.

Some Thoughts

All the changes in classes and teachers take some adjustment. They don't just happen automatically. If you stay informed about what's happening with your child at school, you'll know when your help and guidance are needed.

4

THOUGHTS AND BELIEFS

New Kinds of Thinking Skills

You hear the following kinds of questions either once or often:

"Why do I have to make my bed? I'm just going to sleep in it again tonight."

"I read this poem over three times, and I don't see anything in it about death. What is the teacher talking about?"

"Why do I have to have a curfew? Don't you trust me?"

A Closer Look

J ust as early adolescence is an age of physical, emotional, and educational changes, it's also a time for some important changes in the way kids think.

New kinds of thinking. One of the most important of these changes is that, in the language of the psychologists, young adolescents move from concrete thinking to a more abstract kind of thinking. In other words, they develop the ability to do a lot more thinking "in their heads" than younger children.

A common example is the case of the younger child who sees the moon as being about the size of a dime. To the younger child that's how the moon looks. But the older child can understand that the moon is quite a bit bigger than a dime. The older child understands (just by thinking about it) that the moon is a long distance away.

You can actually see changes in your child like a growth spurt or muscle development. You may not notice, however, that your child's thinking has become more sophisticated and complex until the change has long since happened.

New attitudes toward authority. In addition, young adolescents frequently go through a change in their attitudes toward authority. As children, we generally acquire most of our beliefs from authorities we respect (usually our parents). Someone tells us something, and if we accept that person as an authority, we tend to believe what we're told.

Later on, as our minds develop, usually during the early adolescent years, we start to form new identities. Some experts say that developing a new identity and a sense of independence is the most important thing that happens during adolescence. Young adolescents may begin to question beliefs that they have always held and authorities they have never questioned before. They may have to have some proof about things they've always taken on faith.

Every adolescent experiences this to one degree or another. It goes hand in hand with adolescent rebellion, which is also normal. The process can be unsettling, both for the adolescent and his or her parents and teachers.

What makes this change difficult for everybody involved is that young adolescents need authority, direction, structure, and firmness in their lives—even while they may seem to be fighting them. Without the presence of carefully handled authority, young adolescents tend to border dangerously on chaos when they start to "test the limits."

Changes in values and ideals. Another change has to do with values, ideals, and fairness. As reflected in the questions at the beginning of this section, many young adolescents develop a serious interest in such issues as justice, fairness, and integrity. At an earlier age, these issues weren't so important. Justice was what some authority said it was. Everything was yes or no, right or wrong, black or white. But now it isn't that simple.

The young adolescent wants and needs to see concepts like justice and fairness translated into action. He or she often asks surprisingly intelligent questions about how decisions are made and rules are defined. Probably more than youngsters at any other age, early adolescents expect the adults they care about to demonstrate the virtues they want demonstrated. They also tend to expect adults they admire to be absolutely perfect. When adults disappoint them, they can be critical and intolerant.

Sometimes we may get the impression that they're watching closely and waiting for us to make a mistake. In a way, they are. But, more important, they're starting to become independent young adults with their own sense of judgment and morality.

Some Thoughts

Young adolescents are beginning to think for themselves. Simple explanations won't do. Be prepared to take the time to talk things out and answer what may be some challenging, or at least thought-provoking, questions. A discussion may start out with your child challenging you, but if you stick with it and remain patient, it can be an important time for sharing and communication.

5

SOCIAL CHANGES

The Changing Social Scene

Now that your son is in junior high or middle school, he has a whole new set of friends, and you haven't met any of them.

A Closer Look

This can be a difficult time for parents. Just when you think you've begun to understand all his changes and moods, he changes friends and friendship patterns, and you have to start all over again. To some extent, the changes in school contribute to this. In grade 6 or 7, kids from several elementary schools are usually brought together in a central building. The old elementary school friendships and social circles may break up and change.

All of this can be as puzzling for parents as it is for their children. Usually children—and even their parents—get to know each other fairly easily in an elementary school. The small size of most elementary schools has a lot to do with this. When your child is in elementary school, you feel you have some control over his or her friendships.

But junior high and middle schools are likely to be much larger. Your child has also reached a point where he or she needs to establish some independence. This can be a major adjustment for everyone involved.

Some Thoughts

Early adolescence brings new social opportunities and changes in friendships. It's a time when parents need to "let go" a little and give their children more independence.

There should be a balance between freedom and limits, however. Know where your child is and who his or her friends are. Talk with the parents of your child's friends if you have the chance. Stay in touch.

Social Groupings

You overhear your 13-year-old daughter call your 16-year-old son a "sosch." What does that mean?

A Closer Look

"**S**osch" is just one of many slang words for the varieties of cliques that teenagers form. It's short for "socialites." Don't worry—it could be worse. She could have called your son a "burnout." Every secondary school has these groups. Mainly because of the larger school and the need to belong to a group, for the first time in their lives kids this age may become part of a rather rigid social system—also known as the peer group.

Unfortunately, there may not always be very good reasons why kids belong to different groups. It can depend on something as superficial as an early (or late) growth spurt or certain kinds of clothes. Too often kids get stuck in certain groups and never really get out of them.

Most young adolescents simply aren't prepared for this social screening process. It catches everyone by surprise. Not only are they not ready, but often they don't have the ability to establish themselves in the social circle that might be best for them.

Although the names of the different teenage cliques differ from school to school and area to area, there are almost always at least three main groups. The social order starts with the top kids, or leaders, and goes all the way down the ladder to students who are either unknown to most other students or always in some kind of trouble. Students may call the top group such names as "jocks" or "sosches." They may label the bottom group with such names as "burnouts" or "stomps."

Often the groups in the middle don't have a label. They're just there. Kids in the middle group may try desperately to join the group above them, but if they fail in this effort, they may actually choose to join the group below them.

Some Thoughts

T he groupings and cliques of early adolescence start early and run deep. As a parent, there isn't much you can do about what group your child is in. You should be aware of the situation, however, in case you need to help your child deal with the pain of rejection.

How Important Is Belonging to a Group?

All of a sudden your son has become a loner.

A Closer Look

This is just one example of a common social change that many young people experience in early adolescence, but it carries a powerful message. It may be your son's way of dealing with all the other changes he's experiencing. In order to understand your child, you first have to realize that these changes are happening and that they're a normal part of growing up. He may not like these changes, but they're unavoidable. You can't head change off, and you can't delay it, but you don't have to be trapped by it.

On the other hand, some kids can handle not belonging to a group. They might even be better off. If he has one or two good friends, that could be more important to him than running with a crowd.

Some Thoughts

You can help your child manage the social changes of early adolescence, live through this period of transition, and even thrive. Remember that the peer group is important to young adolescents, and there's nothing wrong with that. Parents are often just as important, however. Don't give up on the idea that you can make a difference.

Part **2**

Building Self-confidence

1

A BASIC INGREDIENT OF SUCCESS

Why It's So Important

Your son, a rather shy boy, draws a three day in-school suspension for smoking in the parking lot.

Your 14-year-old daughter has begun to go steady, and you suspect that she's into heavy petting—at the very least.

Your son tries out for the swim team, but he quits after three days of practice before he's had a chance to see how good he is.

Now that your once-so-gentle son is 14, he has become loud, boisterous, and even rude at times.

Your daughter is making low grades in school, and her teacher tells you that she isn't even trying.

A Closer Look

At first glance you might think that all these different patterns can't possibly have anything in common. Nevertheless, all of them may be connected with the same thing—a lack of self-confidence.

How we feel about ourselves can make a difference in how we act, speak, and even think. Understanding the role of self-confidence—or self-esteem, self-concept, or whatever name we use for the way people feel about themselves—can be important in understanding why people do some of the things they do.

This is especially true of the young adolescent. A 12-year-old boy may be well aware that he's outgrowing his shoes every three months and his voice is cracking, but that doesn't mean

31

he understands what is happening to him. Many children during the adolescent years will spend some time feeling embarrassed, inadequate, and out of it. (Many, of course, will not. Lots of kids make it through adolescence feeling good about themselves and shrugging off such things as cracking voices without any problem.)

Now, a natural reaction might be, "What's the harm? What difference does it make? Life isn't always a picnic in the park. The real world is tough, and kids need to learn that." There is truth to this reaction. Even if we could go through life protecting our children from any kind of hurt, it wouldn't be appropriate to do so. Young people do some of their most important learning by dealing with challenges.

But young people who don't have a strong feeling of self-confidence are a lot less likely to face challenges effectively than those who do. Being self-confident doesn't mean that you have a big ego or an inflated view of yourself. It does involve feeling good about yourself and knowing that you have unique abilities and limitations.

If young adolescents don't have a healthy self-concept, they can overreact to normal problems and become seriously unhappy. Some sobering statistics remind us of this. For example, in the U.S. suicide has become the second leading cause of death among people between the ages of 10 and 14 (3). A lack of self-confidence is also associated with many other common problems of adolescence.

Without self-confidence your child may not have the determination it takes to see tasks through to satisfactory completion. Young adolescents who lack self-confidence also have trouble establishing independence and thinking for themselves. They spend too much time trying to do what they think they have to do to gain the attention or respect of others. This is always dangerous. They're at a point in life where they're about to have some exciting new choices and opportunities. If they aren't self-confident, instead of growing in a healthy way and making good choices, they may spend all their time trying to please others.

Perhaps it's obvious that parents who want to enhance their children's self-confidence should begin to think about this long before their children have reached early adolescence. Still, there are things you can do to help your child develop self-confidence even now—or at least you can help to keep the normal embarrassments and frustrations of early adolescence from being more painful than they need to be.

It's useful to picture self-confidence as being like a three-legged stool. Take away any one of the legs, and the stool will collapse. Each leg is important to keep the stool standing. The three legs of the stool will be examined in the next three chapters. They are:

- Feeling skillful

- Feeling appreciated

- Taking responsibility

Each chapter offers specific suggestions about how you can help your child develop that particular leg of his or her stool.

Some Thoughts

I f we want to help our children experience success in early adolescence, we can begin by helping them develop a positive, optimistic attitude toward life, toward the future, and toward what they can do. It's best to start this process as early as you can, but it's never too late.

2

FEELING SKILLFUL

Nothing Succeeds Like…

After working hard to learn the clarinet for about a year, your daughter makes the school band, and it changes her whole personality. She studies harder, she's pleasant to be around, and she even does her chores without a lot of hassles.

A Closer Look

Sometimes it works just this quickly. Surprising, positive changes happen among young adolescents all the time. The reason is simple. There's nothing that gives a kid a feeling of self-confidence and well-being quite as much as finding out that he or she can master a skill or do something well.

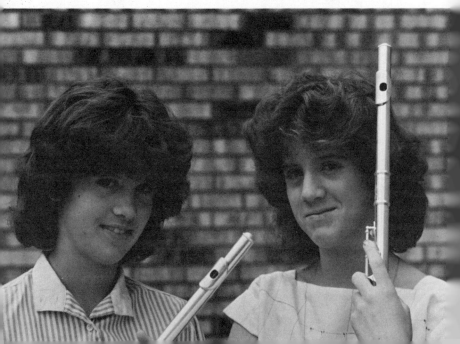

Have you ever watched children who have just learned to tie their shoes? They may sit by themselves for hours just practicing their newly learned skill. Notice the contentment in their faces, the pleasure they get from knowing that they can do something important. It's the same thing for young adolescents. Feeling skillful can change their whole attitude about themselves.

Although young adolescents tend to value some skills more than others (for example, athletic ability and academic achievement), the important point is that kids this age need to feel good at something—anything. It's the sense of competence and mastery that counts.

You may be able to help your child develop a special skill or talent if he or she hasn't already done so. Be on the lookout for things that your child does well. Don't hesitate to notice and to praise. Your praise can be a key element in establishing your child's self-confidence.

Some Thoughts

Before you can do it, you have to believe you can do it. One of the most helpful things you can do as a parent is encourage your child to discover and develop his or her natural talents and abilities.

Recognize Your Child's Skills

Your son has always enjoyed building things more than reading books. Now that he's an adolescent, he really dreads school.

A Closer Look

It's a fact of life: some people are more gifted with words than with their hands—and vice versa. The world needs carpenters and plumbers and mechanics, but the schools are oriented mainly toward people who succeed with words and symbols.

A student who is more comfortable in the nonverbal, physical, or mechanical arena is going to spend a lot of time at school on things he doesn't do very well. That's enough to make anybody unhappy. All of us would rather do the things that are easy for us.

Your boy may not be good at sports or academics, but he still has a special ability. Like everyone else, he needs to use that ability enough to develop feelings of being competent. Since he probably won't get that chance in school, he's going to need some help from you.

What can you do? First, try not to criticize him. For example, a father complained, "How do I get my son to read books? All he wants to do is make radios and other electronic instruments out of spare parts he's always scrounging. When I was his age, I read a book a week, and he hasn't even read one book all summer."

A good response might be, "Love him and bring him more spare radio parts—and maybe even some books about radios." The point is that you can help to strengthen your son's self-confidence. You can even help to direct his interests (for example, radios) toward other interests and skills (for example, reading).

Some Thoughts

Children need to use their abilities regardless of what they are. Judging and blaming your child because he or she isn't strong in areas that you consider important will get you nowhere. It may actually harm your child's self-confidence and your relationship.

Parents Are Teachers Too

You ask your son to start cooking one meal every week in order to help out with family chores. He makes a big mess the first time he does it, and after dinner he says, "I'm never going to cook another meal again as long as I live."

A Closer Look

To achieve competence in any activity, first you have to try that activity. Any time you try something, you run the risk of failing. It hurts to fail—especially if you're in your early teens. People might laugh at you or criticize you. Often, it's just easier not to try in the first place.

At times it seems as if kids this age are almost terrified of failure. The fear comes out in one of two ways. Either they refuse to try new things, or if they do, they want constant feedback about every move they make. Here are some rather typical comments from a middle-school classroom:

- "It isn't fair to ask us to do this. We've never done it before."

- "Can you check to see if I'm doing this problem right?"

- "Yes, I prepared my speech, but I don't feel like giving it."

Young adolescents can't afford the luxury of not trying new things, even when that might be scary. Experimentation is an important part of this stage of life. At the same time, there has to be room for failure. It shouldn't be seen as something criminal. Kids need to learn that it's okay to fail at something, and they should feel confident enough to bounce back and keep trying.

You can help in a couple of ways:

- First, you can help your child master new tasks by breaking the whole task down into parts. Let's use the dinner-preparing experience as an example. You might have had some luck by dividing the task into small sections—for example, beginning by teaching your son how to prepare a variety of dishes separately. This is just good teaching. If you can break a complex task into segments, your child will have a much better chance of putting it all together.

- The second thing you can do for your child is create an atmosphere that takes the sting out of failure. This really isn't all that hard to do. Risk trying some new things yourself. Share your past experiences about how difficult it was for you to develop competence in a skill. When your child tries and fails, praise him or her for trying something difficult in the first place. Ask questions about what he or she is planning to do differently the next time. Let your child know that you still like him or her and that the failure wasn't the end of the world.

Some Thoughts

If we want our children to learn, we have to make room for their failures as well as their successes. One way to help your child achieve big successes is to start with small ones.

Helping Your Child to Overcome the Fear of Failure

Your daughter takes up gymnastics, but when she practices at home, she asks you to watch her and comment after almost every move.

A Closer Look

Either your daughter is a dedicated perfectionist or this is a classic case of "fear of failure." Ask any teacher—all teachers have had students like this. When kids make such a nuisance of themselves, it's hard to fight the urge to scream, "Do it yourself just this once! Where's your independence?"

Screaming at her will accomplish very little except to help you get out some of your frustration. The best medicine for her lack of self-confidence is a taste of success. If you can possibly arrange things so she can achieve something on her own, do so. Then heap praise on her and point out how well she did without any help.

There may be another problem here. Your daughter may be too dependent on your encouragement. "Wait a minute," you might say. "I thought that was what I'm supposed to do. Encourage her, praise her."

As a successful baseball coach once said after a game, "One pat on the back is worth two kicks in the pants." We do need to recognize our children's abilities and successes. We even need to praise them for some of the small things they do that may not seem so important. It's possible to overpraise a child, however. If we're too quick to encourage or if we praise children when they don't really deserve it, we can make them so dependent on our praise that they won't want to tackle anything on their own. When we do that, we've made our children into robots who are totally subject to our control. No parent wants that.

Don't be afraid to praise your child and to lend encouragement and support. But don't overdo it, and don't offer praise when it hasn't been earned. Sometimes you'll notice that just having done something well is so satisfying to your child that he or she doesn't need any reward from you at all. The accomplishment is enough to make your child feel good. That's what the girl worrying about her gymnastics needs. She needs to master a skill completely by herself, and she needs to experience the joy of having done it. Maybe this will get her over that fear of failure enough so she can tackle some new things on her own.

Some Thoughts

According to an old saying, "A job well done is its own reward." Use encouragement wisely and sparingly. Don't make your child dependent on it.

3

FEELING APPRECIATED

You Can Make a Difference

Now that your son has reached his teen years, you have to chase him down to hug him every night, but you can tell that he still enjoys it.

A Closer Look

Don't feel alone. This is just one indication of how much your son wants to be independent from you, which is perfectly normal at his age. Sometimes young adolescents are so eager to be independent that they'll act as if any sign of parental affection or appreciation is babyish. Then when you persist, they really enjoy it.

Every human being needs to feel loved, accepted, and appreciated. To have a strong self-concept, to be in the best mental and physical health, we all need to feel that someone likes us, needs us, and accepts us.

Young adolescents are no exception. In fact, given the many different threats to self-confidence in early adolescence, kids this age may need to know they're appreciated even more than people in other age groups. In their self-doubt, they constantly seek reassurance and acceptance wherever they can find it.

Ideally, you will be your child's most reliable and steady source of love and acceptance. The hardest thing, of course, is to be able to feel loving toward your child even when he or she is in the middle of being angry, upset, and selfishly unaware of you and everyone else. Whatever happens, remember to love your child and demonstrate that love frequently. Equally important, *like* your child. That may seem difficult at times, but try it. You may surprise yourself.

Acceptance is more than saying, "I love you now, but when you get through this difficult stage, then we can really be friends." Acceptance is saying, "I like you. I like the things you say. I like your jokes (even when they're bad). I like who you are."

How do you communicate these things? You watch your children. You go to their ball games. You spend time with them. You talk with them, and you listen while they talk with you.

If you're having trouble making all this happen with your young adolescent, you may want to try some special activities. Think about some things your child likes to do that you can share—building a model, for example, listening to music, or going to a ball game. Even something as simple as walking the dog can be an opportunity to share love and affection together. Let your child know that he or she is worth your time and attention.

If you and your child are anywhere near typical, he or she is going to do some things during early adolescence that will make you very happy. He or she may also disappoint you, embarrass you, and anger you at times.

Those times, more than any others, are when you need to show love and acceptance. Sure, you can love your child when he or she has just brought home a report card with straight *A*s. It's a lot harder, though, to show the same love when teachers call you from school to tell you that your child hasn't handed in any homework since the beginning of the term.

Some Thoughts

If we appreciate our children, they often respond with behavior that makes us appreciate them even more. There's nothing like a spontaneous dose of love and affection for building self-confidence. On the other hand, getting into a cycle of disapproval and blaming can make a bad situation worse. Try to forgive your child's smaller mistakes, and there may be fewer big ones.

The Need for Peer Approval

Your daughter announces, "If you don't let me go to the party, I'll be the only person in school who isn't there. I'll never get invited anywhere again."

A Closer Look

Don't you love that old "make them feel guilty" approach? If she seasons this with a few tears, she may just be able to convince you that you're a bad parent.

Don't give in, however, if you're determined that she shouldn't go. She's just trying to tell you something about herself. Mainly, she needs to be reassured that she's appreciated—not just by you but by her peer group. As far as she's concerned, she won't get the acceptance from her peers that she needs unless she goes to that party.

Who can blame her? Peer acceptance, peer approval, and peer pressure are powerful forces that probably mean more to all of us than we might want to admit. When young adolescents find a slot in a social group in school, they're beginning to discover a whole new life and identity for themselves. Being accepted by their peers is an important part of their feelings of self-confidence. Wanting peer acceptance is a normal and healthy part of growing up. No matter what we may think of our children's friends, we have to recognize their need to be appreciated by people their own age.

On the other hand, peer pressure can have its negative side. Among the possible dangers:

- **Peers are fickle.** They change their minds, their rules, their expectations, and sometimes even their friends as often as their moods change. Regardless of how strong friendships may seem or how established a child may seem to be in a group, friendships among young adolescents can be as shifting as the sands of a windblown desert. This can be especially difficult for the kind of child who prefers to have one close, steady friend.

- **Peers can be cruel.** Often it seems as if they have to tear other kids down just to make themselves feel acceptable. It's not unusual for a whole group to gang up on one poor kid and make him or her the target of all its barbs and teasing. Saying or doing something nasty to this person then becomes almost a requirement of group membership. You're "out" if you show the poor kid any kindness or sympathy. All that cruelty might seem on the surface like some odd kind of teenage playfulness, but bear in mind that it really hurts. If your child relies solely on peer acceptance to feel appreciated, he or she may be in for some rough times.

- **Peers make tough demands.** Probably the toughest part of wanting to be accepted by one's peers is trying to figure out what the peers want. Since peers' expectations are never really written down in a code, most kids just try to guess what's expected of them. This can be dangerous. For example, if your daughter is striving for acceptance and appreciation among the boys in her group, she may engage in petting or heavier sex, thinking that this is expected of her. Some young people abuse their bodies with drugs and alcohol because they think that is expected. Some shoplift and steal, believing that their peers will look up to this behavior and consider it cool.

Some Thoughts

Young adolescents need to be appreciated by their peers. That's normal and appropriate. If they rely too much on peer acceptance, however, they can lose their right to be themselves. Parents have to be careful in discussing or criticizing peers. The best approach is to be knowledgeable about your child's peer group and stay in the background unless you think it's really urgent for you to step in and take some kind of action.

"Hero Worship"

Your son is always talking in reverent tones about one specific boy in his class.

A Closer Look

This is an interesting case of peer pressure—a peer group of one.

Some boy or girl establishes himself as the leader, the standard setter, and everybody in the class, or maybe in the whole school, is suddenly copying the leader's every move.

If this guy unbuttons the second button on his shirt, every boy goes around with his bare chest showing. If this guy gets a shorter haircut, shorter haircuts appear everywhere. If it's a girl and she shows up at school one day with three earrings on each ear, the next day several other girls have imitated her invention.

What should you do if your son succumbs to a case of hero worship for one of his peers? You might begin by getting to know that peer. You might ask your son to invite him over for a meal or to watch a game on TV. You might get to know his values and what he might ask your son to do to gain appreciation. One thing is certain: you won't get anywhere by telling a 13-year-old that his hero is no good.

Some Thoughts

Peer pressure may be as simple as the pressure imposed by one kid. Your ability to resist or control peer pressure as a parent isn't much different in cases like this than it is with a whole group of peers. Whatever you do, keep in mind that although some peers may make you nervous, to your child they're as necessary as food and water.

4

TAKING RESPONSIBILITY

The Need for Independence

Through your influence your son gets his first job mowing lawns around an apartment complex. You drop by to check on his work, and he flies into a fit of rage.

A Closer Look

Sometimes we're lucky that kids this age are creatures of extremes. It would be awful if they stayed as angry as they can get for very long. It may seem strange, but one minute he'll be crying out for independence and reacting against any hint that he might not be mature enough to handle all the responsibility in the world. The next minute he may remind you that he's a child and wants to be treated like one.

He has to go through this. It's part of the maturation process. He has to test his wings. He has to discover if he can fly on his own, and he wants to try it without any interference from you. The irony is that he still wants you there to catch him in case he falls.

Considering his dilemma, his behavior is understandable. He may say to himself, "I'm growing up, aren't I? I'm beginning to look like an adult, and I can handle adult responsibilities." In fact, a few generations ago when each family had a cow to milk, wood to chop, and a garden to till, 12- and 13-year-olds made valuable contributions to their families. Now that we no longer have so many chores to do, there's no economic role for children. If we're creative enough, we may find work for them to do that will make them feel truly responsible and independent. In most families, however, there isn't enough work to satisfy teenagers' needs to feel that someone expects them to behave like an adult.

Coming at a time when they want and need responsibilities, the lack of real responsibilities hurts their self-confidence. Fortunately, this is something we can help them with. Following are some specific suggestions. Although you may not be able to use all of them, maybe they will help you come up with some ideas of your own:

- Find ways to help your child accept responsibility. Show your child how to do his or her laundry or even cook meals. If your child loses something, make him or her find it or replace it.

- Assign your child some chores and expect them to be done. You may get an argument at first. Most children protest chores even though chores are a vitally important part of character building. Don't allow your child to refuse to do chores. You're still the boss of the house, and you are doing this as much for the child as for the family. Also, expect the chores to be completed to your satisfaction. If they aren't done right, don't yell or threaten. Establish a set of reasonable and logical consequences. Eventually you'll get across the idea that the chores must get done. It's important to follow through with your requests and be consistent in your expectations.

- Discuss family rules with your child. Be clear in explaining which rules are not open for negotiation and which ones are. If it seems appropriate, negotiate.

- If you can afford to give your child an allowance, do so. Calculate how much money you would ordinarily give him or her over a week or a month. Then let your child be responsible for all of his or her expenses during that period of time—for example, lunch, bus fare, and extras. Don't offer additional handouts unless you think there's a very good reason for them. If your child blows it, he or she will just have to go broke like the rest of us.

- Help your child find a job that will fit into the school and family schedules. Delivering newspapers at 6:00 a.m. may not be a guarantee of financial or personal greatness, but a lot of successful, happy adults spent their adolescence doing it.

- Act as if you trust your child. If your child breaks his or her word or doesn't keep your trust, discuss the incident, and then forget about it. Don't keep a mental record of offenses. In the process of growing up, we all make some mistakes, and we all need opportunities to start over again.

Some Thoughts

If we give our children responsibility because we trust that they will be able to handle it, we have helped them to develop a healthy sense of independence and self-confidence. This might require us to stand by at times and not say anything while we watch them trip and fall, but it's the only way they can begin to develop a sense of competence and mastery.

Building Trust Through Responsibility

When you remind your daughter of the ten o'clock curfew on week nights, she pleads, "Everyone else gets to stay out later. Don't you trust me?"

A Closer Look

I t seems that every parent hears these words at some point. They, too, grow out of the need to feel responsible and in control. Although you really haven't done anything to attack that feeling, and you haven't expressed doubt, she is so sensitive about it that she reads you wrong. In fact, she may be trying to assure herself that she really is responsible enough to know when to come home.

Keep reminding her anyhow, even if she does scream. You won't be damaging her self-concept, but you will give her a sense of clear expectations.

Then, when she does come home on time, you can praise her for her responsibility and her trustworthy behavior. You can let her know that the more trustworthy she is, the more responsibility and independence you'll give her. Eventually she'll be ready for a later curfew and other responsibilities. Make it clear that all you're doing is giving her an opportunity to earn your trust.

Some Thoughts

E ven though a child needs to know that she's old enough to go out in the rain, she may still need for you to buy the umbrella. Building trust is one of the most important steps in helping your child become independent and responsible. Try to assume that your child is trustworthy as much as you can—that way, you'll be creating a positive expectation that may be fulfilled.

Part

3

*How To
Talk Together—
and Listen*

1

UNDERSTANDING

Getting Through

You used to be able to talk with your daughter, but now that she's 13, she wants to be alone all the time. When you do talk to her, either she's sullen or you wind up shouting at each other.

A Closer Look

There may be some serious hidden problems here, but the most likely explanation is that we have a classic example of a breakdown in communication—a common occurrence in families where there are young adolescents.

It's sad that this happens so often, because early adolescence is a time when your child could really benefit from some adult wisdom and insights. Yet it's more likely that communication between parent and child breaks down at this age instead of improving. When your child really needs you, he or she doesn't know how to communicate that need, and chances are you won't know how to begin to rebuild the relationship.

Young adolescents often blame their parents for these failures of communication. They accuse them of not listening, of not being interested, of not understanding. On the other hand, parents usually blame their children. They accuse them of being rude or sullen or secretive.

But all this blaming doesn't do anybody any good. In fact, maybe the breakdowns in communication could be avoided or lessened a bit if everybody stopped blaming each other long enough to achieve a little understanding.

That's what this section is about—establishing and improving communication.

Communication is far more than the words you use. It's the art of relating effectively to others. It's the art of breaking down the walls that too often separate people and building bridges that help relationships to flourish.

The following chapters look at five aspects of communication:

* Understanding

* Appropriate Timing

* Listening

* Identifying Feelings

* Touching

Some Thoughts

Learn how to communicate effectively, and you'll have mastered one of the basic elements of building a good relationship with your child. Remember, though, that communication takes work—it doesn't always happen naturally.

Understanding the Teen Culture

You buy her a record for her birthday, but she takes it back the next day and trades it for another. You can't tell the difference between the one you bought and the one she bought.

A Closer Look

Adolescents have a culture all their own, complete with their own literature, language, music, art, and activities. Apparently, you don't understand it. Of course, as an adult, you can't really be a part of that culture. You wouldn't want to.

It's actually a good arrangement. Adolescents need something that belongs especially to them. This gives them a sense of identity and independence. But the culture gap can become a real wall at times between you and your young adolescent. Since you are the adult in the relationship, you can't let that happen. Although you may never understand the adolescent culture itself, the important thing is to understand your child's need to have a special culture.

Once you've achieved this understanding, you need to choose your areas of disagreement carefully. Although you may never understand why your daughter chose her record instead of yours, you can at least understand her need to do it. And if her choice of music, reading, or TV programs isn't immoral or indecent, probably it's not worth disagreeing about. Don't let an issue as insignificant as music build a wall between you and your child.

Appearance and dress are the same kinds of issues. Although we don't always understand why they want to wear their hair that way or why they think green fingernails are an absolute necessity, we can understand their need to look "okay" in the eyes of their peers. Again, unless your child's appearance gets downright shoddy or indecent, protesting may not be worth the sense of misunderstanding it will create.

Regardless of how different you think the two worlds are—yours and your child's—there are still some areas where the two of you can meet and share mutual interests and ideas. If you want to maintain open communication with your child, find those things you can share and use them as a means of understanding the rest of his or her world.

Some Thoughts

Adolescence has a special culture. We may never understand it, but if we want to communicate effectively with our children, we should respect the need for it. However you handle this issue, be on the alert for signals from the teen culture that may be negative and harmful to your child—for example, pro-drug movies and songs. Let your child know that you're concerned about these "danger signals" and he or she ought to be concerned too.

2

TIMING

Communication Can't Always Be Scheduled

You realize the need to maintain communication with your son, so you schedule a weekly meeting with him. He never says anything at these meetings, but he always wants to talk just before he goes to bed.

A Closer Look

Scheduling a certain time each week to talk to your child may be needed in an age when everybody is so busy. In fact, some schools even schedule special times for students to meet with teachers.

The idea is a good one, particularly if your schedule makes it difficult for you to spend time with your child. Scheduling a specific time to be together every week is an important reminder that you care and that you take his or her joys and problems seriously.

Don't be discouraged, though, if your son can't think of anything to say during these scheduled times. Life doesn't always happen on schedule, and a young teenager may not always be able to talk about it on schedule. For your son, life is a moment-by-moment adventure. He may be excited about something in the heat of the moment, but ten minutes later he may have forgotten what it was that excited him.

Another point to remember is that he probably hasn't learned the kinds of communication skills you would expect from an adult. He may feel awkward sitting down with you just to talk. He's at an age when he may be feeling awkward about everything. Still, he is probably grateful for your attention. Young

adolescents often want and need to talk with their parents, especially about sensitive issues and things that are bothering them.

The important point is that you made the effort of scheduling the meeting. Even if the meeting seems awkward, something good is going on just because it's taking place. Notice that he does want to talk later. That's a good sign.

Keep having your weekly meetings. Act as if you look forward to them, enjoy them, and profit from them. Make him think the meetings are as much for him as for you so they won't seem like just another one of your scheduled obligations.

Also, try to keep the meetings informal. This can be the best way to open communication. You might just go out for a hamburger together. You might share the shopping chores and then stop for a soft drink on the way home. If you don't make too big a deal of the meeting, your child is more likely to relax and open up to you.

Some Thoughts

Demonstrating caring and commitment through our behavior can be as important as any words. Just being with your child may be an important form of communication even if you don't say very much.

When the Timing Is Wrong

You finally get up enough nerve to have that heart-to-heart talk with your daughter about sex. When she gets home from school that day, however, she's crying and refuses to tell you why.

A Closer Look

Just what you needed! Sometimes it seems as if kids think they're the only ones who have communication problems. Obviously, it never occurred to your daughter to think about how hard it might have been for you to muster enough courage to initiate that talk in the first place.

Talking about sex might not always be so difficult, but clearly you've chosen the wrong time to do it. You might never have known it was the wrong time unless you'd tried. Something is bothering your daughter that makes communication about the subject difficult and painful. It's best to drop the topic for now and bring it up again at another time.

Some topics for discussion demand clear heads and cool spirits. In this case, you were planning to share some information, but probably you were also hoping to teach some values. To teach these lessons effectively, you need a strong foundation of good feelings between the two of you. If, for some reason, one of you isn't feeling thoughtful or reasonable, don't choose such a time for an important discussion. You won't be successful.

Other sensitive topics, in addition to sex, that will require a calm, open, and trusting atmosphere are honesty, responsibility, drug and alcohol use, the quality of schoolwork, and family rules. All of them are highly emotional issues that require a level-headed approach.

Some Thoughts

Timing is an important part of communicating with young adolescents. What's essential is that you learn how to read their moods so you won't be working against the current. Find the right time and then make the attempt. Since good timing can't always be arranged, be alert to informal opportunities for communication and make the most of them.

3

LISTENING

It's Okay to Ask

For the last several days your child has seemed to be pre-occupied with something. You have no idea what it is.

A Closer Look

How often we get ourselves in trouble just because we don't use the most obvious methods of communication! If you want to understand your young adolescent and keep the communication open, one of the best ways to start is to learn the simple art of asking good questions.

It really isn't very difficult. Often it's the best method imaginable for getting the information we need if we want to understand our teenagers.

Most questions you might want to ask can be divided into two categories: those that are easy to answer and those that aren't. Easy questions are the ones that ask for information or facts. Examples might be:

- Your friends haven't been over lately. Have you asked them?

- Where were you this afternoon?

- What are your plans for the weekend?

- Did you do your history homework?

- What did you have for lunch today in school?

If your child knows the answers, he or she can respond quickly. If not, your child can at least tell you that he or she doesn't have an answer. Be aware too that some of these questions might be slightly threatening to your child's sense of independence. You

may have trouble getting satisfactory answers even to simple questions.

The difficult questions are those that ask about feelings, moods, and opinions. These questions often begin with "why?" Examples might be:

- Why did you do that?

- Why do you feel that way?

- Why do you want to go to the party?

Those are tough questions to answer. With a young teenager, the chances are excellent that the answer you'll get is "Because."

Although it may be important to ask the tough questions before you've finished a discussion with your child, it's better to begin with the simpler kind.

Don't be afraid to use questions to help your child tell you what it is he or she may be having trouble telling you. If you notice a pause or a moment of hesitation, ask, "What did you say then?," "What did she do?," "How did you feel?" (The last one will work best if you use it after the conversation has already begun and your child is fairly comfortable.) Asking such questions serves two purposes. It tells your child that you're interested in listening, and it encourages him or her to keep talking. At the same time, it helps you get the information you need.

Some Thoughts

Y ou don't need to put your child on a witness stand. Ask questions that make it easy for him to answer.

Get the Whole Story

The principal calls and tells you your son was fighting at school. When he gets home, you make him go directly to his room. Then you follow him in, shouting about all the trouble he causes.

A Closer Look ·

I t's damaging to act as if we're afraid of our children or fail to take action when some action is called for. And action is probably called for here. Whether you approve of fighting or not, fighting in school is wrong. This is a serious situation, and you do need to take care of it.

The problem is that you didn't stop to hear his side. You didn't give him what's generally considered a basic right in our society, the right to a fair trial, the right to be heard. Although you may not change your mind at all after you've heard the details of his side, you still need to listen. You need to let him know that your decision to punish him is based on all the facts and information—that you've been as fair as you can be.

Once you've heard his side, you might decide that, at least to some extent, he was in the right. Fighting in self-defense, for example, might have been justified.

If his story doesn't match what the principal told you, you have another kind of problem. You now have to probe a little deeper. This isn't to say that your child might lie to you, but some have been known to do it. That's why it's so important for you to hear his explanation of exactly what happened. You need that kind of information to make the right decision.

You could turn this situation into a profitable learning experience. Even if you decide you still have to discipline him after you've heard his story once or several times, he'll see that you're trying your best to be fair. For some reason, kids can accept discipline better when they know the punishment is fair.

Listen to his story from start to finish, and assure him that you understand the reason he made his decision to fight. Then make it clear that he made the wrong decision (if this is what you conclude) and explain why.

If you can convince him that you're trying to be fair in all this, you just may build some communication bridges. Who knows? Next time he may weigh the consequences a lot more carefully before he decides to fight.

Some Thoughts

When we get our children to talk, we might not like what we hear. However, if we listen carefully enough, we may be pleased in the long run. Even when you're upset and angry about something your child has done, one of the best things you can do for communication, both now and in the future, is take the time to talk it out calmly and sensibly.

Giving Your Undivided Attention

Your daughter tries to talk to you while you're feeding the baby.

A Closer Look

If anyone is entitled to your full attention, surely it's your own child. But in this case you can't give it to her. You have to feed the baby. Explain that to her. Tell her, "Look, I really want to hear what you're saying, but if I don't feed the baby, she's going to scream so loudly that I won't be able to hear you anyway. Wait just a minute until I'm finished. Then I can give you my full attention." An explanation like this is just common courtesy.

Another reason you need to give your daughter your undivided attention is that you may need to help by asking good questions. That takes concentration. Good communication will involve some effort from both of you. Over the long haul of parenthood, however, it's definitely worth the effort.

Some Thoughts

All of us want the spotlight for a while. Give it to your child, and you'll be helping him or her to shine.

4

FEELINGS

The Need for Understanding

Your daughter comes home crying. The boy she has a crush on didn't look at her on the bus. You have a hard time hiding a chuckle.

A Closer Look

Sometimes the way young adolescents react can be downright funny—or maybe just annoying. The temptation can be not to take them seriously because they can act so grown-up one minute and so childish the next. It's hard to know which is the real person.

No matter what we may think about how our children react to things, they have real joys, real pleasures, real hurts, and real heartaches. Although their feelings may not always make sense to us, they're still just as real, intense, and important as ours.

Since our children have lived only 10 or 12 years or so, they haven't had enough experiences to make good judgments about what is important and what isn't. But their feelings are still important to them. If you want to communicate effectively with your daughter, you have to begin by understanding that. You may think her reaction to the behavior of the boy she likes is funny, but it isn't funny to her.

Communication is more than hearing what she says. It's also understanding how she feels—and letting her know that you understand.

Understanding feelings and letting your child know that you understand may be the hardest part of communicating with an adolescent. It's also one of the most important.

Now, back to the situation at hand. More than anything else, your daughter needs your understanding. She doesn't need

71

you to tell her she's silly for crying. She doesn't need to hear that she'll get over it. She simply needs someone who will understand—and who will let her cry.

Some Thoughts

Our children's feelings are likely to color our communication with them. It's best to let the child do the coloring. The important thing is that we see the whole picture. Pay attention to your child's feelings. They may be more important than anything that he or she says.

It's Not Always Easy to Tell

You come home and slap your son on the back as you always do, but he pulls away.

A Closer Look

Reading someone else's feelings can be a challenge. We can't see feelings, and most of the time other people can't explain their feelings very well, especially young adolescents. So it's hard to know sometimes what is going on under the surface. On the other hand, it's easy to observe behavior. He pulled away, he slammed the door, she hugged you, she smiled. Those things are clearly visible.

In order to be successful in communicating with our kids, we have to learn to look beyond their surface behavior and make some guesses about what might be going on inside.

Every behavior is a form of communication. When a boy uses drugs, he is saying something about his feelings. When a girl quits trying in school, she is saying that something is bothering her. When your son vacuums the living room without being told, much less threatened, he's telling you something positive. If your child comes up and hugs you for no apparent reason, you know something is going on—it might even be that he just felt a sudden burst of affection for you.

In the case of your son pulling away because he's in a bad mood, the best thing you can do is respect his feelings and back off.

Since he wants to be left alone, respect that. If you have a good relationship with him, he'll get close to you again as soon as he feels more sociable. You will make a lot more progress with him if you ask him about his bad mood when he has had some time to get into a good mood.

Some Thoughts

There is no magic decoding ring that will help us read a young adolescent's feelings. Rather, what we need to do is put out our antennae in the hope that we'll pick up the right signals.

Anger—and ''I Feel'' Statements

When you get angry with your daughter, she always accuses you of hating her.

A Closer Look

Although this bothers you when it happens, you still have to give her some credit for a clever defense. She may not even know for sure what she's doing, but if she can make you look like an ogre, she can take some of the heat off herself for whatever she did that made you angry in the first place. It's a good trick if she can pull it off. (It can also be infuriating and make you even angrier.)

There may be something you can do to bring some balance to the situation. For starters, it won't help to shout at her and then, when she accuses you of hating her, get even angrier. Obviously, that hasn't worked for either of you.

The first thing to do when you feel yourself getting angry is to stop for a moment and think about it. Maybe you're not expressing your anger clearly. Maybe you're misdirecting it. You may be more hurt than angry.

Anger is a legitimate feeling, and it's all right to express it, but you need to express your anger in such a way that it doesn't become a devastating attack on your daughter. If you can yell louder than she, you may be able to control the situation for the moment, but you really won't do much to correct what disturbed you to begin with. In other words, you won't really be communicating.

A good approach to expressing any feeling, including anger, is to let your child know how you're feeling by stating it as simply and directly as you can. One of the best ways to do this is to begin your communication with "I feel… ." This is called an "I Feel" statement. For example, you can just tell your daughter, "Right now, I really feel angry with you. I don't hate you. I asked you to do something. And you didn't do it. Now, I feel angry."

Using "I Feel" statements is a far more effective way of communicating your feelings than the old pull-out-the-stops-and-yell routine. She still may accuse you of hating her, but if you try some "I Feel" statements, you're making progress.

Once you have mastered that, try "catching" her doing something you approve of. Find a time when you're really feeling happy to be her parent and express that feeling with an "I Feel" statement. Don't be afraid to tell her that you feel proud or happy. If you make a point of expressing positive feelings at least as often as you express negative ones, you'll be on the road to good communication with your child.

Some Thoughts

Not expressing your feelings is like keeping a tight lid on a boiling pot. Eventually the pot will boil over, and then you'll have a real mess. "I Feel" statements can help you lower the heat. U.S. President and statesman Thomas Jefferson said that if you're angry, the best thing to do is count to ten before you say anything—and if you're very angry, count to a hundred.

5

TOUCHING

Reach Out...As Much As You Can

Your son is looking sad, so you put your hand on his shoulder. In turn, he rests his head on your shoulder.

A Closer Look

You are really cheating yourself as a parent if you think that the only way to communicate is with words. We communicate through feelings and expression and all sorts of nonverbal ways. One of the strongest forms of communication is through the simple, time-tested method of touching.

It's easy to do once you get the hang of it. You don't need any special rules. And it's as effective as any form of communication you can use.

Of course, some families are more physically affectionate than others. If you commonly and easily hug your child or put a hand on his or her shoulder or shake his or her hand, there really isn't any need to stop just because he or she has reached that advanced stage called adolescence. If you aren't accustomed to displays of physical affection, it isn't too late to start.

Now that he is a teenager, your son may act as if he doesn't need the communication of touch anymore, but don't believe it. You may not want to embarrass him by making a big deal out of it in public or in front of his friends, but just remember that touching is a powerful communication tool.

You need all the communication tools you can use during this time. When the natural barriers of adolescence begin to develop as your child seeks his or her independence, do everything you can do to keep them from becoming impenetrable walls.

Some Thoughts

Young adolescents are often unsure about parental love, as they are about so many things. Touching helps provide assurance of that love. It's particularly effective after a fight or conflict.

Part **4**

The Family — Getting Along Together

1

THE FAMILY FIRST

The Family Teaches Values

Since you're really concerned about teenagers using drugs, you hope your daughter's school has a good drug education program.

A Closer Look

I f you're fortunate, maybe your daughter's school does have a drug education program. It might even be a relatively good one. In fact, some schools are doing a fine job of teaching young people about drug and alcohol abuse, given the limits of what schools can do. It would be great if your daughter could participate in such a program. Don't expect the school to do the whole job, however.

Regardless of how good schools may or may not be, how good teachers may or may not be, or how serious your daughter is about school, the family is still the most powerful educational institution we have.

If you want your daughter to learn about drugs and alcohol, at the very least you should know what the school is teaching. That way, you will know how to supplement what your daughter is learning in school by doing your own kind of teaching at home.

This doesn't mean that you should set up drug education classes in your living room. The family has a responsibility, however, for some forms of education that are as important as any class.

The family can teach such lessons as respect for authority, a healthy self-concept, a desire to learn, and a system of positive and healthy values. The school can and should attempt to teach

all of these things. But it's in the family setting, starting in the earliest stages of childhood, where children really learn them best.

The teaching of values is a good example. If a child uses alcohol or other drugs, has casual sex, lies, cheats, steals, or doesn't work to the best of his or her ability, those are ways of expressing values. He or she is making choices about how to behave, and values are an important element in these choices. Your daughter might have learned some of her values in school. She might have learned some of them from her friends or even from TV and movies. But she definitely learned part of her value system from you.

That should not come as a surprise, even though you may not remember talking to her about values. She learned by watching you, imitating you, and trying to do what she thought she needed to do either to please you or hurt you, depending on her mood at the moment. (Sometimes, in case you hadn't noticed, kids will do the opposite of what they know their parents value. It's a common part of adolescent rebelliousness and the move toward independence.)

In short, the family unit is one of your child's most important teachers. It may be a family unit of two people—a parent and a child—or it may be a two-parent family with several children. Whatever kind of family you have, the lesson of what you value is something your child will learn just by watching what you and the others in the family do.

Some Thoughts

Children can be straight *A* students when it comes to learning values from their families. Parents have a responsibility to make certain that they're teaching the right kinds of lessons. Don't assume, however, that your child knows what your values are in relation to alcohol and drugs and other things about adolescent behavior that may become a problem. Talk about these things; make sure that your child understands your values. Also, find out what the school is teaching about alcohol and drugs and other sensitive topics.

The Importance of Being Together

Although your kids seem to fight all the time, you still take the whole family on a camping trip. Everybody has a great time and talks about it for months afterwards.

A Closer Look

You hear this kind of story often. This is what families are all about—togetherness.

But after all that fighting at home, you might wonder—what made the difference? What miracle occurred?

Another way of looking at this is to ask, "What is the glue that holds our family together?" It's a valid question.

We might all like to think that families are welded together by some mysterious, natural force, but that isn't true. Just look at the statistics. Almost one-half of all marriages in the U.S. end in divorce. Most likely a lot of others are often on pretty shaky ground. Unfortunately, in far too many families today there is no glue holding the family members together.

Why is this so? The lawyers and judges throw around terms like "incompatibility" or "infidelity." Those are just fancy words for explaining that these families don't have any glue holding them together.

Think about it. What is the glue that holds your family together? What are the special things that the members of your family have in common and are loyal to?

If you don't have any good answers to those questions, take some time to ponder them. Now that you have a child who is a young adolescent, it will be time well spent. Adolescence can put quite a strain on the glue that holds your family together.

In the past, families were glued together by such things as the family farm, the home, the father's occupation, the neighborhood church, relatives, or just survival itself. Now that we all move around so much and the nature of work has changed so dramatically (more and more, both parents work full-time outside the home), those things simply aren't available to most of us.

Today families have to look for glue in other places and situations. One of these could be a family vacation. A good vacation with some interesting new locations and adventures can be exactly what a family needs—a common experience of pleasure and fun. It can work wonders. It doesn't have to be expensive either. It can be a simple camping vacation, or even just a weekend away together.

If you can't take a vacation, other things might work: a common hobby, a pet, active family membership in a church or synagogue, eating meals together, a favorite television show that all of you watch together, building something together, painting or decorating a room, or having a special family night each week. There's no end to the different possibilities.

Every one of these experiences or events can help to glue your family together. This is vitally important if the family is going to provide the kind of environment where a young teenager feels a sense of support, identity, and love.

Some Thoughts

Maybe the best glue is contact cement. Spend some time together. One way to make the most of this time is to have different family members contribute ideas about what you will all be doing during your special time. That way, it won't just be one family member telling the others what they ought to enjoy. If you have more than one child, give each one a chance to contribute ideas and suggestions. Make "special family time" as important in your weekly schedule as getting the chores done.

2

DISCIPLINE

Steps for Solving Problems

You tell your son that taking out the trash every night will be one of his regular chores. He starts to argue that he shouldn't have to do it, that his younger sister ought to do it, and that he's too busy to take on more chores.

A Closer Look

This kind of reaction is a lot more normal than many of us would like to think. It gets at one of the fundamental concerns parents have about their children, especially during the adolescent years: discipline.

One explanation is that your son's behavior may be a test. It may be his way of probing the limits of your authority. It may also be a strong statement of his independence—another way of testing your authority.

Your first impulse might be to match force with force, stubbornness with stubbornness. You're bigger than he is, and you have a right to tell him to do a job without any backtalk. The problem with this approach is that force by itself won't work for very long, especially with a young teenager. You may be able to use force to restrain or control your kid while you're looking at him, but it won't be much good once he's out of your sight.

You might as well recognize now that what really controls people isn't authority but respect for authority. If your boy doesn't respect your authority, you may force him to take out the garbage, but you haven't changed his attitude, and you really haven't corrected the problem.

A fairly common approach to problem solving might work here. Many teachers use these steps all the time to resolve conflicts they have with students about such things as expectations, rules, or even punishments. Here's how it works:

- State the problem.

- Ask questions that will help to clarify the issues on both sides.

- Examine various alternatives for solving the problem

- Decide which alternatives that are consistent with your values best solve the problem.

- Choose a solution that allows both sides to "win."

The final step is probably the most important. It shows that you aren't using your authority in an arbitary manner. Instead, you understand that the best way to resolve a problem or conflict is to satisfy both sides. That way, both sides will respect, or "buy into," the solution.

How would this process work in the case of your son's not wanting to take out the garbage? Here is an example:

- Wait until calm has been restored, and then state the problem. That's simple. You want him to take out the garbage, and he doesn't want to do it.

- Ask (or discuss) questions that will help to clarify the issues on both sides. Somebody has to take out the garbage. He says he doesn't have time. Maybe the discussion can go a little deeper than that. Maybe you've been asking him to do things lately, and his response has been to refuse or dis-obey—or turn the conversation to why his little sister isn't being asked to do the same things.

- Examine various alternatives for solving the problem. You could get a goat (a little humor can go a long way in relieving the tension of situations like this). You could empty the garbage yourself and deduct the "cost" of this chore from his allowance.

- Decide which alternatives solve the problem best. Probably the goat is out.

- Finally, if it's at all possible, agree on a plan both of you can live with. That way, neither of you will feel that he has lost the battle completely. If you can work this out, you can keep your authority, and your son can keep his self-respect. One way of giving him some say in the matter would be for him to decide exactly when he will empty the garbage.

Bear in mind that this process won't solve all the problems that might come up in your family. It isn't a cure-all, and it may not work every time. It will work often enough, however, to make it worth your while to try it.

There is one clear advantage of solving problems this way instead of trying to use the force of your authority: it will help you keep down some of those walls that can quickly destroy communication between you and your teenager.

Some Thoughts

You are the authority in your house. Wear your authority comfortably. Being prepared to compromise in cer-tain matters is an important way of maintaining your authority. The key is to know how to maintain the right balance between compromise and direction. Clearly, there are times when your word has to be law.

Teaching Your Child How to Live With Consequences

Your daughter has gotten into the habit of leaving her bike out in front of the house whenever she's not using it. You like the front of the house to look clean and orderly. It's getting to be a real problem.

A Closer Look

This may not be the worst problem you ever have while your child is an adolescent (if it is, lucky you!), but it offers a good illustration about a simple way to establish discipline within the family.

One of the most effective strategies for "disciplining" children is to get them to learn self-discipline. What you really want is for your daughter to put her bike away when she's finished using it without your having to issue the order. To get into the habit of doing this on her own, she has to know that it's important and she has to want to do it. This is where consequences come in.

Teaching children about consequences is one of the most important things a parent can do in establishing discipline. There are two kinds of consequences: natural consequences and logical consequences. A natural consequence might be that your daughter's bike will get rained on or possibly even stolen if she leaves it in front of the house for days at a time. The consequence is a natural result of her behavior, and she'll learn an important lesson just by observing what happens.

A logical consequence is something that you impose as a parent, but it's a consequence clearly related to the behavior you're trying to change. For example, you might make it clear to your daughter that if she leaves the bike out front one more time, the consequence will be to spend an hour or so picking up things around the house that other people haven't put away. There's logic to this consequence, and your daughter is likely to make a connection between the consequence and the behavior you are trying to correct. Cleaning up after other people's carelessness is a lot more logical than saying, "If you leave your bike in front one more time, you can't watch TV for a week."

Some Thoughts

One of the best ways to teach a child self-discipline is to let the child see the consequences of his or her inappropriate behavior. Parents can guide their children toward appropriate behavior by knowing when to let them learn through natural consequences and when to impose logical consequences.

Keeping Things in Perspective

A mother gets upset when her daughter comes in late, so she grounds her for six weeks. Later she calms down and realizes the punishment is too harsh.

A Closer Look

We're all guilty of something like this at times. First, look at the mistakes the parent made. She didn't get her daughter's side of the story. She didn't give her a chance to participate in a decision that would be both fair and effective. She didn't tell her daughter how she felt about the situation. She simply relied on her power of authority.

Now she is in the position of either abiding by a bad decision or apologizing to her daughter and backing off from the punishment. She might say, "What? Apologize to my child? Admit that I'm wrong? Won't that undermine my authority and destroy her confidence in me completely? If I apologize, what can she expect from me in the future?"

Let's face it, young adolescents are old enough to know when a punishment is fair and when it's handed down in a fit of anger. They're also old enough to be treated like intelligent people.

In this case the daughter was wrong in coming in late, but the mother was wrong in overreacting, and she owes her daughter an apology. Apologizing won't undermine her authority. Instead, it can help to build a bridge between the two of them.

The mother might tell the daughter something like this: "I'm sorry. I didn't mean to get so angry and suggest such a harsh punishment. Now that I'm feeling calmer about it, I need you to understand that it really upsets me when you come in late. I get worried when you're out after curfew and I don't know where you are. What you did was wrong. And it requires some kind of consequence. Maybe we can talk together about what an appropriate consequence would be." Saying something like that sure is a lot better than losing your temper.

Some Thoughts

When our children are wrong, we have a right to expect an apology. When we're wrong, our children have the same right. Children don't learn to say "I'm sorry" freely and comfortably until they have experienced the good feelings this simple act can generate.

The School's Authority

Because of an argument with a teacher, your son gets sent home from school and can't come back until you go with him.

A Closer Look

This is a tough situation. Those teacher conferences can make a parent feel like he or she is in elementary school again and has just been caught throwing rocks on the playground.

But there are some real possibilities here. If you handle this situation correctly, you could teach your son an important lesson. If you make a mistake, it could be costly.

This is, in short, a test of your ability to teach your son the proper attitude toward authority. Regardless of what you try to teach, you're probably going to teach him to look at authority just about the way you do.

The first step in solving the problem is a matter of good communication. You need to listen to your son's side of the story. You need to hear him out.

Unless something really out of the ordinary happened at school, he probably made a mistake. Even if he had a good

reason for the argument, his behavior was out of line. He carried things too far.

Try to sit as calmly as you can and hear his story. It will be helpful too if you can make him realize that he played some part in the situation. Try to make him aware that whatever happened, you're willing to hear his side of it.

Reason with him and explore alternatives. If he had a legitimate reason to disagree with the teacher, how could he have done it without losing control and getting suspended? If he didn't have a legitimate reason to argue, what else was going on? What were his feelings? What's been bothering him about school—or about this particular teacher? By being willing to listen, you can let him know that you haven't completely turned your back on him and judged him wrong, even though he behaved inappropriately.

Once you've had the discussion, you still need to go to school with him. This is one of the less pleasant tasks of parenthood, and there's an art to it.

Try to approach it with the attitude that the school is on your side. The teachers and administrators don't want to harm your son. All they want him to do is develop the proper respect for authority. Presumably, you and the school have the same objective—to help your son make it through early adolescence and grow into a responsible person. Since you and the school are partners in this project, you need to let your son know that the two of you are cooperating.

With your son present, assure the school officials that you and your son have talked about the matter. Explain that the two of you have agreed on how he should have handled the situation. This should satisfy the school's requirements, but, more important, it could help your son learn appropriate respect for authority.

Some Thoughts

Schools and parents usually have a common purpose. We can help our children understand how to handle authority in their lives if we let them know that.

When Kids Test the Limits

Your daughter has been gone all afternoon, and you have no idea where she is. This is the third time this week it's happened. You're angry and worried.

A Closer Look

Clearly, your daughter is testing the limits. In fact, she's gone far beyond them.

Since this kind of thing happens in thousands of homes every year, let's take a look at how the situation got out of control.

Probably the first time she came home late, you were so relieved to see her that you greeted the offense with a mild reprimand of some kind. But what did you do the second time? Whatever you did, somehow you didn't get the idea across that there would be serious consequences if the same thing happened again.

One of the hardest things a parent sometimes needs to do with a young adolescent is set limits and clearly spell out the consequences for misbehavior—and then follow through immediately if that form of misbehavior occurs.

None of us likes the disciplinarian role. It's a lot easier

just to retreat or shrug off our child's misbehavior—or even pretend we didn't notice.

But let's be straight about it: your child needs for you to set limits and then to follow up with reasonable consequences when those limits are violated. Without those limits and consequences, your child will get the idea that anything goes. Especially in early adolescence, kids who think that anything goes will often go wild.

Some Thoughts

Sometimes setting limits is one of the most loving things you can do for your child. Make it clear what the limits are and what the consequences will be for violating those limits. Your child may say you're being "mean," but don't believe it.

3

CONSISTENCY

Why Consistency Is So Important

You get a big promotion, so you decide to move into a new house far away from where you've been living just as your daughter is about to enter junior high school.

A Closer Look

People between the ages of 10 and 14 are experiencing all kinds of changes. They encounter changes everywhere—in their bodies, their friends, their schoolwork, their voices, and even in their families.

It's ironic, isn't it, that just at the time when your child is dealing with one adjustment after another, a major adjustment happens in the family as well.

It could be any kind of change. You may get a new job or move to a new neighborhood or even a new city. Something may change in your marriage. You may have another baby. You too are at a time of life when there might be some important changes. Many of the changes you're experiencing, like the move to a new house, might be positive changes. You have a right to enjoy them.

The important thing to remember is that changes in your life may place extra burdens on your young adolescent. These changes may seem positive and wonderful to you, but to your child they may be terrible.

Any move that requires a young adolescent to change schools can be devastating. At best it's extremely difficult for a child to find acceptance in the social circles of a new school. Besides, if she's already made the adjustment to a number of different teachers, a move to a new school will require her to adjust to a whole new group of teachers.

If you have to move, or if your family undergoes any other significant changes, the best thing you can do is be sensitive to your daughter's need for consistency in her family life. Try to maintain as much consistency as you can. For example, while you're still in your old house, develop some family ritual like everyone eating breakfast together.

Whatever happens, your daughter needs a sense of consistency at home, because at this particular time she isn't going to get that sense in many other areas of her life.

Some Thoughts

When everything in our children's world is changing, it helps to have a home to depend on. Even the simplest things can make an important difference—for example, saying "Goodnight" every night with a kiss and a hug or taking a moment to talk about how the day went. It can also help to establish and maintain ties with other families, a church or synagogue, relatives (even if they're far away)—anything that will provide clear values and stability.

Establishing Some Ground Rules

Your daughter wants to go to a party, so she asks you for permission. When you say no, she asks your spouse.

A Closer Look

This is the old "play them against each other" trick. Kids have been using it since the beginning of recorded history.

You can't let her get away with it, especially when she's at

this vulnerable and impressionable age. Early adolescence is a time when kids are doing a great deal of testing and experimenting in many different areas of their lives. It's essential that their parent (or parents) be as consistent as possible in every decision.

How can you avoid the problems that occur when your child is constantly trying to get you to change your position from one day to another? Try this: make sure that well in advance you determine your views on some of the crucial issues that are bound to come up as the years progress. Let's start with a list like the following:

- **Dating.** When can she start and what are the rules? How are you going to supply the information about sex?

- **Curfews.** What will they be, and what will the consequence be for broken curfews?

- **Grades.** What are your minimum requirements, and what will you do if your child doesn't meet them?

- **Friends.** What will you do if you don't like her choices?

- **Family chores.** What will your child be required to do, and what will the consequence be if she forgets?

- **Clothes and appearance.** What are your non-negotiable requirements—boundaries that will be necessary to help her in directing her choices?

- **Her room.** Do you demand inspection rights? Must you knock before entering? Will you let her decorate in her own unique way?

- **Music.** How loud, how late, and what kind?

- **Movies and TV.** How much, at what time, and what kinds?

- **Family activities.** When does she have to be with the rest of the family, and when can she stay home by herself?

- **Jobs.** Will she be allowed to work? Will you insist on it? What kind of work will she be allowed to do?

- **Drugs and alcohol.** Who is responsible for providing reliable information? What will you do if you suspect she's experimenting? If you find out for certain?

This list should help to get you started. You can add to it as other ideas come up, but at least if you get answers to these questions, you will have worked out some of the major issues. If you develop a consistent position on important issues, your daughter will realize that there are clear, firm family rules and limits. You'll be amazed how this can prevent problems.

It's even better if you involve your child in developing the rules and the consequences of violating them. That way, your child will know that he or she had a part in making the rules and will be more likely to respect them. They won't be seemingly arbitrary restrictions handed down from above.

Some Thoughts

As parents, one of the best gifts we can offer a young adolescent is consistency. Make sure that the rules in your family are clearly stated and that your child acknowledges and understands the consequences of violating them. It will help to get the rules down in writing. These steps can avoid misunderstandings and problems later on.

4

EXPECTATIONS

Accepting Our Children for Who They Are

You're a gung-ho tennis player, and you encourage your son to join the school team. He isn't as good as you'd like him to be.

A Closer Look

Many of us can probably understand this father's feelings. We put so much time and love and energy into raising our children that we can hardly be blamed for wanting them to be everything they can be. Yet sometimes parents go too far; they expect their children to live out their own fantasies.

It's especially important to be aware of our expectations of our children when they reach early adolescence. This is the time when kids really begin to come into their own and establish an independent identity.

Early adolescence may be the time when we realize that our children aren't exactly what we wanted them to be—that they're not the super scholars or musicians or athletes we dreamed about. They may succeed at things in which we're not even interested. We may realize as they grow more independent from us that our dreams aren't their dreams.

We have to have some expectations for our children. If we don't, there won't be any standards at all, and we won't know whether they're cheating themselves and their own potential by working below their capabilities. Our expectations have to be based on what our kids can realistically accomplish, however—their talents, likes, and dislikes, not just our ambitions for them.

In communicating your expectations to your children, try to think in terms of three basic principles:

- Develop a set of expectations that are appropriate to your child's abilities.

- Check with your child to see what his or her own expectations are.

- Communicate your expectations clearly; don't make your child guess.

You may want to make a real project out of talking to your child about expectations. Try getting together for a goal-setting session. This is easier than it may sound. Pick a time when you and your child are feeling good about each other. Then ask some questions that will start him or her thinking. Here are some examples:

- Let's look ahead 15 years or so. You'll be about 30 then. What do you see yourself doing?

- Where would you like to live? What kind of house and family would you like to have?

- What do you want people to think about you? Do you want them to think you're honest or hard-working or wise or rich (or all of these)?

- What do you think you'll need to do to reach your goals?

Don't be too disappointed if the session doesn't lead to some clear decisions. Asking a young teenager to look far into the future is a challenge at best. But your questions can set the whole process in motion. Chances are you'll get enough information to help the two of you begin to develop some realistic expectations based on your child's abilities and interests.

Some Thoughts

Being 14 is hard enough. A child that age doesn't need the added burden of carrying his parent on his back too. Children do need to know, however, that their parents are involved in their lives and that they care.

Part

*Alcohol and
Other Drugs—
Some Questions
and Answers*

1

THE PARENT'S ROLE

The Reality of the Problem

You're out at a neighborhood party. Many of the other guests are parents of kids who go to the same school as yours. During the evening you overhear several people talking about drug and alcohol use at the school. Your child has just started grade 6, and this is the first time you've heard about the problem. You've been dreading this moment for years.

A Closer Look

We all wish it weren't true, but the fact is that children today grow up in a world that strongly influences them to be interested in alcohol and other drugs. The influence of the media alone (especially television) starts children thinking from the earliest days of childhood that one way to be attractive, healthy, and happy is to put a pill in your mouth or drink something. By the time children get to their early teens, most of them are well aware of other teenagers who use alcohol and other drugs. The temptations are everywhere.

The use of legal drugs—mainly alcohol and tobacco—is part of our culture. Although more and more people disapprove of smoking and recognize its dangers, alcohol and tobacco can be bought almost anywhere by adults. It's impossible to protect our children from advertisements that show these drugs in a favorable light.

Because so many adults smoke and drink—and seem to have quite a good time doing so—young adolescents tend to see the use of these drugs as part of being grown-up. Many kids (but not all) want to try alcohol and other drugs as soon as they can. Often they don't see much difference between legal drugs and illegal ones (for example, marijuana and cocaine). Just as often, of course, they are tremendously ignorant about the effects of all kinds of drugs.

An important step in dealing with the problem of alcohol and drug use among youth is to recognize it for what it is—a major health problem of epidemic proportions. Here are some facts revealed by a variety of recent surveys:

- Children are experimenting with drugs and alcohol at much younger ages than a decade ago, frequently as early as the upper elementary grades (4).

- By the time they reach grade 12, the majority of students have tried alcohol, and nearly as many have tried marijuana (5).

- Alcohol is by far the "drug of choice" among adolescents, mainly because it's so easy to get (6).

- Most children learn about drugs and are offered drugs the first time by their friends (7).

- One of the major concerns of youth today, according to a Gallup poll, is dealing with alcohol and drugs (8).

The last statement is at least somewhat encouraging. If you're worried about the drug problem—well, so are kids! Recent surveys show that young people are beginning to recognize that alcohol and other drugs are a serious threat to their well-being. In fact, research has shown that drug use is declining among students in the U.S. because young people are more aware of the serious health hazards than they used to be (9).

Unfortunately, the message may not be getting through clearly enough to younger teenagers. Moreover, far too many teenagers continue to use alcohol and other drugs, and the use of cocaine has been steady among students in their last year of high school (10). The fact that some forms of drug use are declining from their extremely high peaks of a few years ago is no reason to be complacent.

Most young teenagers know of people their age or somewhat older who are involved with alcohol and drugs—whether it's their friends, their older brothers or sisters, or brothers or sisters of friends. Unless you're ready to move to the North Pole and throw away your TV and radio, there's no escaping the influence of alcohol and other drugs. You probably wouldn't even escape it at the North Pole.

Some Thoughts

Our children will have to make their way in a world that's filled with opportunities to use alcohol and drugs. We can help them by understanding what they're facing, talking with them about the problem, keeping communication open, and preparing them to say "No" when the opportunity to use alcohol and drugs arises. The best way to start is by openly accepting that alcohol and drug use are problems you can't avoid just by wishing they weren't there.

Who Is Vulnerable?

A good friend calls you in a terrible state of worry and anxiety. Her child has just been suspended from school for possession of a small amount of marijuana. You breathe a sigh of relief, knowing that the same thing couldn't happen to your own 14-year-old because she's doing so well in school and she's involved in so many after-school activities.

A Closer Look

You're probably right about your daughter, especially if you're close to her and know her well. Nevertheless, drug and alcohol use are problems that can affect many different kinds of young people—even those who seem on the surface to be "okay."

Research shows that teenagers get involved with alcohol and drugs for many different reasons. Most important among them are:

- Peer pressure to use

- A willingness to take risks

- Curiosity

- Parental use of alcohol and other drugs

- Lack of self-esteem

- Problems at home or school

- Being frequently bored

- A family history of chemical dependency (11)

Your daughter may not have any of these qualities. Don't assume, however, that everything is okay and you have nothing to worry about. All children in our society are vulnerable to the pressures to use alcohol and drugs. Research shows that most adolescents—no matter where they live, whether it's the inner city, a suburb, or a rural area—will eventually be faced with an opportunity to try chemicals. Usually this will happen within the peer group.

What makes the drug problem especially worrisome is that there are no guarantees that your child will not be harmed. Just because parents abstain from drinking, for example, does not mean that their children will follow suit. Your child may seem as happy and normal as anyone, and then within a few months become seriously drug-dependent. There are no guarantees of any kind. It would be wonderful if someone invented a vaccine against drug and alcohol abuse, but that may never happen. Drug and alcohol abuse are complex problems that have no simple solutions.

Some Thoughts

Youthful drug and alcohol abuse can happen anywhere to anyone. It's impossible to predict with certainty. All you can do is try your best to prevent it and reduce the risk to your child.

Some Facts You Should Know

As one parent put it, "I know that kids in our school are using alcohol and drugs. And I also know that my own kid is drug-free. I just wish I could stay sure of it and not have to worry all the time."

A Closer Look

The point is so important that it's worth repeating: there is no surefire way of guaranteeing that your child won't

become involved with alcohol or drugs. There are plenty of things you can do, however, that other parents have found successful in preparing themselves—and their children—to deal with the problem.

One of the most important is to be as well informed about drug and alcohol use among youth as you possibly can. This isn't the place for a long listing of all the various drugs young people use. (See the resource section for places where you can get reliable information.) Besides, you don't need to become an expert on drugs. You do need to know at least a few basic facts. Here are some that you should be aware of:

- Alcohol, tobacco, and marijuana (cannabis, pot, weed) are the chemicals that young people use most frequently, and each one is dangerous in its own way. Adolescents who go on to harder drugs usually begin by using one or all of these drugs, which, for that reason, are often called the "gateway drugs."

- Yes, alcohol is a drug. Alcohol is especially dangerous because it's so available and socially acceptable among adults. Children just can't wait to start feeling "grown-up" by using it. There is tremendous pressure throughout the society to drink alcohol, and even though it's illegal for children, the message is getting through to them loud and clear. How many times every night does your child see a TV commercial for beer or wine in which the people are healthy, vigorous, successful, and having a good time surrounded by friends while they drink? Think about it.

- Adolescents who drink alcohol are much more susceptible to serious problems with alcohol, and are likely to have problems much sooner, than adults who drink (12).

- Although alcohol drinking is widely accepted (except for minors), alcohol is associated with half of all automobile accidents and fatalities. Alcohol is also responsible for a variety of harmful diseases and health problems, including cirrhosis of the liver and birth defects (13).

- Young teenagers often smoke cigarettes to feel more grown-up. Yet adults have begun in recent years to kick the tobacco habit while 12-14-year-olds continue to take it up. One reason for this is that teenagers tend to think that they're immortal. To a 13-year-old girl—who is more likely to smoke daily than a boy her age—health problems resulting from cigarette smoking are just for old people (14).

- The marijuana generally consumed today is at least ten times stronger than it was in the late '60s and early '70s, when so many young people first began to smoke pot. Obviously, someone is getting good at growing the stuff. This fact ought to alert you to a potential danger. Although you might have known something about drugs ten years ago, your knowledge may be outdated at a time when you need to be able to tell your children the facts.

- THC, the active ingredient in marijuana, is stored in the fatty tissues and organs and can stay in the body for up to a month. Thus, any person smoking marijuana once a week is actually building up an accumulation of THC that can have harmful effects on the body long after the person has smoked marijuana (15).

- Although doctors and researchers aren't sure of all the health effects of marijuana, there is growing evidence that marijuana can be extremely harmful, contrary to what people once thought. It can have serious negative effects on the immune system, the respiratory system, the reproductive organs, and all other important body functions (16).

- Marijuana, cocaine, alcohol, and other drugs can have a profound effect on a young adolescent's physical, intellectual, spiritual, and emotional development. A Canadian survey of 9-, 12-, and 15-year-olds found that users of alcohol, marijuana, and cigarettes were much more likely than nonusers to have lower self-esteem and negative attitudes toward parents and school (17).

- During adolescence a child should be developing important coping skills for dealing with anger, stress, disappointment, loneliness, and other feelings and challenges. These skills cannot be learned when young people attempt to "solve" problems by using chemicals. A child learns to deal with stress by dealing with it, not masking it with alcohol or other drugs. Stress, loneliness, anger, and disappointment are human conditions. How a young person learns to deal with them is what growth and development are all about.

As a parent, you need to be aware of information like this and continue learning as much as you can. Just knowing this information won't protect your child from drugs, however. You need to take your knowledge and your concern a step further.

Probably the most important thing you can do to keep your child away from drugs is to make a clear statement that in your family the use of any chemical substance for nonmedical reasons by any child is not acceptable.* Then you need to be prepared to back up that statement. As with other disciplinary measures, one way to be prepared is to draw up a list of carefully thought out consequences—and then follow through at the first indication that your rules have been violated. This is not one of the rules that you should "negotiate" with your teenager. It should be absolute and nonnegotiable.

Some Thoughts

Drug abuse prevention begins in the home. Educate yourself with basic information, and take a clear stand on alcohol and drugs. This won't guarantee that you'll never have a problem with your child, but it's a lot better than saying "I know my child won't get into trouble with drugs and alcohol because he's basically responsible" or, worse, saying "Anything goes." Make your expectations absolutely clear. If you think writing them down will help, do so. Then keep them posted for all to see and acknowledge.

*In some families and cultures the use of alcohol by minors may be acceptable with parental permission under carefully controlled circumstances such as family ceremonies and religious occasions. Clearly, such occasions would be an important exception to the general rule.

2

INFLUENCES

All in the Family

You drink regularly and moderately, but you're an adult and your drinking is well under control. You tell your daughter not to touch alcohol until she's of legal age and mature enough to know what she's doing.

A Closer Look

Our children learn more from what we do than what we tell them. This is particularly true of their use of chemicals. A parent may not have a drinking problem as such; lots of people manage to control their drinking. But any parent who drinks regularly is modeling a form of behavior. In effect, the adult is teaching the lesson that drinking is okay, that it's appropriate for adults—and maybe even one of the rewards of being an adult.

Children are far more likely to smoke if their parents do. People who drink are more likely to have children who drink. People who use other drugs are more likely to have children who use other drugs. Many researchers maintain that genetic and hereditary factors may lead to alcoholism and other drug problems.

Maybe your family is the exception. Maybe you're such a good communicator and teacher that you can teach your daughter not to want to drink, no matter what you do, but that's unlikely. A parent's behavior is a powerful influence.

Some Thoughts

For a parent, teaching is the same as living. While your child is in his or her adolescent years, you may want to

113

change some of your own behavior regarding the use of chemicals such as alcohol and tobacco. For example, if you've ever wanted to give up smoking or go without that nightly cocktail, you couldn't choose a better time. Make sure if you do it that your child is well aware of the example you're setting. Even if you think you can't change this behavior, make it clear to your child that you would like to change it if you could.

The Influence of the Teen Culture

One Saturday morning when your son is out, you stop to look into his room. You shake your head in amazement at the weird images in the posters on the walls and in the magazines. "What's next?" you ask yourself. "One of those crazy haircuts . . . or drugs?"

A Closer Look

As mentioned earlier in this book, the teen culture is an important part of adolescence. It's not necessarily a bad thing. Unfortunately, however, the teen culture isn't always a positive influence on kids either. Sometimes it can seem like some kind of monster that wants to take your child away from you. You have reason to be concerned about it.

Children today are living in a confusing time. Often their music and their heroes reflect that confusion. And often their heroes act out the anger and frustration that many young people feel. It's even more unsettling, of course, when their heroes promote the use of alcohol and drugs. So many children have a good deal of spending money today that they've become an easy target for people who may not have their best interests at heart.

You may feel that the music and other symbols of your child's generation are something from another universe, but the best thing you can do is try to get to know them a little bit. For one thing, they may not be as bad as you think. Not all rock musicians are drug users, contrary to the general impression of them. Some have taken a strong stand against alcohol and drug use, just as some have promoted it.

Make an honest effort to tune in to your child's heroes and symbols. If you're concerned about these powerful influences, at least your child will know that you cared enough to try to understand his or her world. It could be the beginning of some common ground between the two of you. You may even discover that you don't really have that much to worry about after all.

Some Thoughts

It won't hurt to get acquainted with the teen culture. Listen to the words of the songs. You might even ask your child if you can go with him or her to a rock concert. Stay alert, and you'll have fewer unpleasant surprises. Keep in mind, moreover, that some of the messages from the "adult" culture can be just as corrupting as any in the teen culture. Your child is probably exposed to at least as many ads for alcohol and cigarettes each day as harmful lyrics of popular songs. Call your child's attention to the many different ways in which these media messages can be harmful to one's health.

Peer Pressure

Since you don't know your daughter's crowd very well, you're afraid that her friends will lead her into drugs.

A Closer Look

Good thinking. You should be concerned about the crowd your child hangs out with. Worrying about it won't do a bit of good, however. Instead of worrying, take action. If you don't know your daughter's friends very well, make a special effort to meet them—and their parents.

Invite them over to your house some weekend afternoon. Get to know them. Although you may not be having as much of an influence on your daughter's decisions and behaviors as you used to, at least you can understand something about her friends and how they influence her.

The peer group is a critically important influence in a young person's decision to use drugs or alcohol. In some groups there's much more pressure to use than in others. Still, your daughter is the most important factor. If you have prepared her to say "No" to drugs, if she's had some actual practice in saying "No" (for example, through a program in school), and if you have made it clear what the consequences of drug use will be, chances are that she'll choose a more positive peer group that doesn't regard drug use as the "in" thing to do.

Some Thoughts

The crowd does make a difference, but your child can learn to say "No" to negative peer pressure. Your child may assure you that he or she has no intention of trying drugs and at the same time be quite vulnerable to negative peer pressure. As much as you can, bolster your child's resolve with praise, agreement, understanding, and support.

3

WHAT IF IT HAPPENS?

How Can You Tell?

One mother who had heard about drug use among students at her daughter's junior high school realized that the problem was serious. She had also heard about kids who were so successful at covering up their drug use that their parents didn't find out until they were heavily involved. "How will I know if my daughter is using drugs?" she asked.

A Closer Look

It's important to know what to look for if you suspect that your child or others in your child's crowd might be using alcohol and other drugs. Here are some recommendations to parents developed by PRIDE (Parents' Resource Institute for Drug Education), a leading organization in Canada and the U.S. that helps parents become educated about the drug and alcohol problem: *

1. **Does your child seem to be changing emotionally?** Does your child get angry more quickly and with little reason, show less affection, seem to be keeping secrets, demand more privacy? Is he or she increasingly withdrawn or uncooperative?

2. **Is your child becoming less responsible?** Does your child forget to do homework and chores? Is he or she late for school and late coming home?

---

* Adapted from PRIDE (Parents' Resource Institute on Drug Education) parent education materials. For further information contact PRIDE. See the resource section for address and telephone number.

3. **Is your child changing friends, dressing differently, or losing interest in school and school-related activities?**

4. **Is your child harder to talk to?** Does your child avoid talking about the changes in his or her life, refuse to discuss drug issues, defend friends who use drugs? Does your child insist that you are picking on him or her, defend the right to live his or her own life, and prefer to talk about the bad habits of adults?

5. **Is your child beginning to show physical and mental problems?** Is your child frequently confused, out of touch with what's going on, or slow to understand? Does he or she seem more sensitive to touch, smell, or taste or suddenly have a big appetite? Has your child lost weight?

Any of these could be signs that a child is beginning to become involved with drugs.

Some Thoughts

I f you suspect that your child might be having a problem with drugs or alcohol, you need to be more alert to signs of change than ever before. Don't hesitate to be a "nosy parent" if that's what you have to do to get the information you need. Your child's future may be at stake. It's important to respect your child's need for independence, but no child has the "right" to ruin his or her life.

Actions to Take

A neighbor tells you that he saw your 13-year-old smoking marijuana with some other kids at a nearby shopping center.

A Closer Look

Discovering that your child is using alcohol or other drugs may be the beginning of a difficult time. On the other hand, you may be able to get through even this trauma of adolescence with your family and your relationship with your child intact. The initial discovery may alarm you, but it doesn't have to be the end of the world. Part of the outcome will depend on your attitude and behavior.

Whatever you do, don't panic! Don't hide your head in shame. Don't scream and shout and overreact. Stay as calm as you can.

The first thing you need to do is sit down and talk with your son about your discovery. Remind him of your rules about alcohol and drug use, and, if you think it's appropriate, follow through now with a consequence.

You may decide to give him a second chance. Maybe this was an isolated instance that won't be repeated. Let him know, however, that you will have to watch him more carefully and that he will need to win back your full trust. Be willing to listen to his side, but don't accept any denials of drug use without careful questioning.

Another step you may want to take is to call all the parents involved. Be sure you inform your son of this decision. Don't be surprised if some of the parents refuse to believe that their children might be using drugs, and be careful not to accuse their children. Make it clear that, for the moment, your main concern is that you believe your son is involved and the rest of the group may be involved as well. If you want, get the group of parents together so you can share information and support each other.

Agree to stay in touch and set guidelines that will be mutually observed.*

In the meantime, keep talking with your son. As calmly as you can, discuss his behavior. If he admits that he's using marijuana, try to help him understand in clear terms why he's doing what he's doing and make sure he has weighed both the immediate and long-term consequences. Emphasize the serious effects on his health that marijuana can have, and don't accept any statements that it's a harmless drug. He may come back at you with a lot of misinformation about drugs and alcohol. Get some books about drug and alcohol abuse to back up your statements. The most important thing is to keep talking.

Whatever you do, don't ignore the situation or treat the matter lightly. This problem is worth your attention. Your child is worth your attention.

Some Thoughts

Discovering that your child has begun to use alcohol or drugs may be one of the most challenging and difficult experiences you've ever had. Don't delay action. That will just delay a solution.

*For a detailed description of how parent groups have organized in this way, read *Parents, Peers, and Pot,* by Marsha Manatt. This book and its sequel, *Parents, Peers, and Pot—II: Parents in Action,* can be obtained by contacting PRIDE (see resource section).

When a Child Becomes Seriously Involved

"I've been through the whole understanding bit," one mother said, after admitting that her daughter was a heavy marijuana user. "I'm tired of being understanding, and I'm tired of talking. Every other weekend my daughter disappears, and the next thing I know, she's back with her druggie friends. Then after a few days of hanging out with them and doing drugs, she's back home again saying that was the last time she'll ever do it. What do I do now?"

A Closer Look

I t's easy to understand how this parent must be feeling. Sometimes nothing seems to work when a child is having serious problems with drugs, and a parent can get discouraged.

Clearly, this parent has reached a point where some outside help is needed. Parents in this kind of situation may decide to seek the assistance of a counselor who is experienced in dealing with youthful drug and alcohol abuse. They should also talk with other parents who have experienced similar problems. It may be that the child needs to spend time in a treatment center, totally removed from the influence of drug-using friends. Often that kind of drastic action is the only way to get a child off drugs.

One strategy that many parents have used is to make it clear that the child will not be allowed back into the house until some ground rules are established. If necessary, they arrange for the child to stay with friends or relatives while they work the rules out. It's a process that can take weeks and even months. Parents in this difficult and trying situation can also benefit from meeting regularly with a group made up of parents who are having similar problems.

Some Thoughts

When a child becomes heavily involved with drugs, there may be a lot of anger and tears before anyone in the family can start to smile again. It's important, though, that the parents keep on trying. Parents must communicate the message that their child is worth all their efforts. They should hold on for as long as they can, remember the good and happy times the family has had together, talk with others who have been through what they're experiencing, and look forward to the day when their strength, determination, and love will prevail.

WAYS TO PREVENT IT

What Parents Can Do

Most parents would be grateful if they could get a clear answer to a simple question: "What can I do to keep my child from getting involved with drugs?"

A Closer Look

Increasingly, parents are discovering some effective answers to this question. There are a number of things you can do to help your child stay clear. Drug abuse is a complex issue, however, and you need to keep in mind that at the moment there is no magic formula for effective drug abuse prevention. Many ideas are worth trying, but none of them is guaranteed to work.

The basic emphasis of the ideas discussed in this section might be called "positive prevention." Positive prevention is just another way of saying that you're going to give your child the best and healthiest preparation for the challenges of adolescence, including drug and alcohol use, that you can possibly provide.

- As much as you can, establish a close relationship with your child. The average parent spends very little time with his or her children, and most of that is taken up with either nagging them or talking about the details of getting things done (getting up, getting to school, making plans for after school, setting the table, doing homework, and so on). Spend some special time with your child every day just for casual, relaxed communication.

  That special time will help you get to know each other better and build a stronger relationship. It will also help you get to know your child well enough to notice physical, emotional, and mental changes that might be associated with drug or alcohol use.

Developing a close relationship with your child will go a long way in building confidence and trust. Also, it will help you avoid panicking over some bizarre moods or behaviors that just come naturally with early adolescence.

- Don't wait until your child is well into his or her teens to start to build a good relationship. Developing good communication and building self-esteem in your child should begin in the earliest stages of childrearing. It's never too late to start, but the earlier you start, the better.

- Include plenty of two-way communication in that close relationship. Make sure your child knows he or she can talk with you. Regardless of what he or she does, don't shut off the communication channels.

- Encourage your child to get involved in positive activities that give him or her a feeling of competence and help to develop useful and enjoyable skills. You have already read about the three-legged stool of self-confidence—feeling skillful, feeling appreciated, and taking responsibility. Children who are involved in positive, constructive activities and who have a feeling that they can do well in things such as sports and hobbies are less likely to use drugs and alcohol than children who feel they can't do much of anything. Think of these positive activities as alternatives to drugs. They provide a lot of the pleasure and self-confidence that many kids think they're getting from drugs.

Look for these positive alternatives at every turn, and make sure that you're not just pressuring your child to do what you want. It could be Scouts, sports, music, electronics, pets—whatever really interests your child. Stay tuned in to your child and you'll know. (Be careful, though, that you aren't programming your child into so many activities that you hardly ever see each other.)

- Talk with other parents of young adolescents whenever you have the chance. Get together informally and share information. Build a support group. It's useful to do this even when you're not worried about any serious problems. When parents are "together," children often have a satisfying sense of stability and consistency.

- Provide as many other support systems as you can for your child. Friends, relatives, a church or synagogue—all can help to make your child feel more secure and self-confident.

- Do whatever you can to meet your child's emotional and psychological needs. We all have these needs, and if we sat down and thought about them, we would probably come up with a list like the following:

  — The need to be noticed. All of us need someone to notice that we exist and have feelings and thoughts.

  — The need for acceptance. We need to feel that someone enjoys our company and likes to be around us. This is especially important for young adolescents at a time when most kids are busy putting each other down.

  — The need for independence. We all need to feel that we're capable of making at least some of our own decisions and that we can accept and live with the consequences of those decisions. You can help your child recognize when he or she is making decisions, encourage him or her to make healthy decisions, and make sure that he or she accepts the consequences of those decisions.

  — The need for love. Some people are perceptive enough to know when they're loved without having to be told. But others need reassurance. Just to be on the safe side, why not get into the habit of regularly telling your child that you love him or her and enjoy his or her company? Maybe a spontaneous hug will get the message across even better. It may be the single most important thing you can do to help your child deal with the challenges of the early adolescent years.

  An important point about the love you give your child is that it should be unconditional love—love without strings attached. "Get As in school and I'll love you" and "Behave and I'll love you" are strings. The message you need to get across is that you love your child no matter what he or she does and that even if you don't like your child's behavior (it may be totally obnoxious at times), you still love your child. It's that simple—and sometimes it's that difficult.

These are common human needs. All of us, including your child, do what we have to do to get as many of our needs fulfilled as we can. If your child can fulfill enough of these needs within the family, he or she won't have to depend so much on the peer group.

Some Thoughts

Your child's best defense against drug abuse is a loving, supportive family. It's in the family that kids can get the help they need to build a strong foundation of self-confidence and well-being for the future.

Put the period of early adolescence into the perspective of a lifetime. Whatever happens, your child is going to spend only about three years of his or her life in early adolescence.

Regardless of the struggles, cherish these years. Hold on to the memories. Keep as many mental or real pictures of them as you can.

Also, cherish your understanding of this occasionally awkward time—and of your young adolescent's varied moods, experiments, and failures.

Never lose sight of the fundamental love and joy that can help both of you look back someday on a special and wonderful period in your child's life.

NOTES

1. National Institute on Alcohol Abuse and Alcoholism. "Conference Report: Runaways and Alcohol." Rockville, MD: National Institute on Alcohol Abuse and Alcoholism, 1974.

2. *Young Adolescents and Their Parents.* A survey conducted by the Search Institute. Minneapolis, MN: Search Institute, 1984.

3. National Center for Health Statistics, Public Health Service. *U.S. Health.* Washington, DC: U.S. Government Printing Office, 1980.

4. Weekly Reader Publications. *A Study of Children's Attitudes and Perceptions About Drugs and Alcohol.* Middletown, CT: Weekly Reader Publications, 1983.

5. Johnston, L., Bachman, J., and O'Malley, P. *Use of Licit and Illicit Drugs by America's High School Students: 1975-1984.* Washington, DC: U.S. Government Printing Office, 1985.

6. Ibid. Also: *The Journal,* June 1, 1985, p. 11.

7. Polich, J.M., Ellickson, P.L., Reuter, P., and Kahan, J.P. *Strategies for Controlling Adolescent Drug Use.* Santa Monica, CA: The Rand Corporation, 1984.

8. The Gallup Organization. Gallup Youth Poll. Princeton, NJ: The Gallup Organization, 1984.

9. Johnston, L., Bachman, J., and O'Malley, P. *Use of Licit and Illicit Drugs by America's High School Students:* 1975-1984. Washington, DC: U.S. Government Printing Office, 1985.

10. Ibid.

11. Norem-Hebeisen, A. and Hedin, D. "Influences on adolescent problem behavior: causes, connections, and contexts." In *Adolescent Peer Pressure: Theory, Correlates, and Program Implications for Drug Abuse Prevention.* Washington, DC: U.S. Government Printing Office, 1981.

12. Smith, G.M. and Fogg, C.P. "Early Precursors of Teenage Drug Use." Paper presented at the 82nd Annual Convention of the American Psychological Association, September 1974.

13. U.S. Department of Health and Human Services. *Alcohol and Health.* Washington, DC: U.S. Government Printing Office, 1983.

14. *Directional Paper of the National Program to Reduce Tobacco Use in Canada.* Ottawa: Consultation, Planning, and Implementation Committee, 1987.

15. Mann, P. *Marijuana Alert.* New York: McGraw-Hill, 1985.

16. Ibid.

17. King, A.J.C., Robertson, A.S., and Warren, W.K. *Summary Report: Canada Health Attitudes and Behaviours Survey, 9, 12 and 15 Year Olds, 1984-85.* Ottawa: Health and Welfare Canada, 1985.

ACKNOWLEDGEMENTS

This book was developed and written by Cliff Schimmels and Hank Resnik in cooperation with noted experts on youth and families. Our thanks to the following people for their assistance:

Tom Adams
President
Just Say No Foundation
Walnut Creek, California

Robert Andringa
Education Consultant
Englewood, Colorado

Sue Andringa
Parent and Homemaker
Englewood, Colorado

Pat Barton
President
Naples Informed Parents
Naples, Florida

Peter Benson
President
Search Institute
Minneapolis, Minnesota

Kathy Burt
Teacher
Great Bend Public Schools
Great Bend, Kansas

Jeanette Cannon
Lions Clubs International
Oak Brook, Illinois

Allan Cohen
Executive Director
Pacific Institute for
Research and Evaluation
Bethesda, Maryland

Jack DoBush
Western Canada Coordinator
Lions-Quest Program
Lamont, Alberta, Canada

Christine Donahue
Member, Resource Review
Committee
National Federation of
Parents for Drug-Free Youth
Berkeley, California

Phyllis Erney
Middle School Special
Education Teacher
Gainesville, Florida

Tom Erney
Psychologist and Writer
Gainesville, Florida

Luther Ford
Teacher
Gary Public Schools
Gary, Indiana

Hal Gaddis
Executive Director
National Middle School
Association
Columbus, Ohio

Bonnie Greene
Private School Teacher
Findlay, Ohio

Ken Greene
Private Christian School
Administrator
Findlay, Ohio

Glenna Gundell
Board Member
National PTA
Piscataway, New Jersey

Tom Hanely
Coordinator of Junior High
Education
Department of Education
Fredricton, New Brunswick,
Canada

Anne Hoover
Director
Quest/*Project LEAD*
Ft. Wayne, Indiana

Mary Jacobson
Past President
National Federation of
Parents for Drug-Free Youth
Omaha, Nebraska

Barbara Johnston
Coordinator of Health and
Physical Education
Ministry of Education
Toronto, Ontario, Canada

Lynn Kemerait
Coordinator of Prevention
Services
Green Street Center
Rutherfordton, North Carolina

Jim Kielsmeier
President
National Youth Leadership
Council
St. Paul, Minnesota

Fannie Layne
Teacher
Cleveland Public Schools
Cleveland, Ohio

Dale LeFever
Assistant Chairman
Department of Family Practice
University of Michigan
Ann Arbor, Michigan

Joan Lipsitz
Former Director
Center for Early Adolescence
University of North Carolina
Chapel Hill, North Carolina

Jane Lorenz
Member, Resource Review
Committee
National Federation of
Parents for Drug-Free Youth
Deerfield, Illinois

Joyce MacMartin
Home Economics/Health/
Family Life Education
Consultant
Department of Education
Winnipeg, Manitoba, Canada

Don Melnychuk
Psychologist
Edmonton Public Schools
Edmonton, Alberta, Canada

Anne Meyer
Executive Director
Deerfield Citizens for Drug
Awareness
Deerfield, Illinois

Linda Millar
Teacher
Ottawa, Ontario, Canada

Roberta Mohr
Child Development Specialist
Columbus, Ohio

132

RESOURCES

ORGANIZATIONS AND CLEARINGHOUSES

Canada

Canadian Federation of Home/School and Parent-Teacher Associations
323 Chapel Street
Ottawa, Ontario K1N 7Z2
613/234-7292

Promotes public education programs on drug use and abuse, and has identified smoking prevention as a priority.

Health Promotion Directorate
Education and Training Unit
Health and Welfare Canada
4th Floor, Jeanne Mance Building
Tunney's Pasture
Ottawa, Ontario K1A 1B4

Can provide information on health-related programs for youth. For publications call 613/954-8576.

Parents' Resource Institute for Drug Education
PRIDE Canada
Thorvaldson Building, Suite 110
College of Pharmacy
University of Saskatchewan
Saskatoon, Saskatchewan S7N OWO
800/667-3747

Has established a network of parent and youth groups across Canada, conducts a national conference, has a speakers' bureau and toll-free information line.

Also see the list of suggested local resources for Canada and the United States.

United States

Center for Early Adolescence
School of Public Health
University of North Carolina
Suite 223, Carr Mill Mall
Carrboro, NC 27510
919/966-1148

Specializes in research and programs relating to the young adolescent age group. Offers a variety of publications and a newsletter.

Families in Action
3845 North Druid Hills Rd., Suite 300
Decatur, GA 30033
404/325-5799

Publishes "How to Form a Families in Action Group" ($10). Operates a drug information center and publishes a regular newsletter.

Focus on the Family
50 East Foothill Blvd.
Arcadia, CA 91006
818/445-0495

Provides references to Christian counselors and parents throughout the country who are concerned about the family. Publishes a monthly magazine.

National Federation of Parents for Drug-Free Youth
8730 Georgia Ave., Suite 200
Silver Spring, MD 20910
800/554-5437

Assists parents throughout the country who are concerned about teenagers' use of drugs by forming local parent groups, conducting an annual conference, and publishing a regular newsletter. Provides information and support to parents who want to "get involved." Nearly every state has a "state net-worker" who will assist in starting other local parent support groups.

National PTA
700 North Rush St.
Chicago, IL 60611
312/787-0977

Has made drug and alcohol abuse prevention a high priority. Offers a variety of informational materials and suggestions to support parents in developing effective prevention programs.

Parents' Resource Institute for Drug Education (PRIDE)
Robert W. Woodruff Building
Suite 1216, Volunteer Service Center
100 Edgewood Ave., NE
Atlanta, GA 30303
800/241-9746

Conducts an annual international conference, publishes a variety of materials, and operates a toll-free information line.

LOCAL RESOURCES FOR ASSISTANCE WITH DRUG AND ALCOHOL PROBLEMS IN CANADA AND THE UNITED STATES

(Check your local telephone book for addresses and phone numbers.)

Al-Ateen. Support and self-help for teenagers from families in which other family members are alcoholics.

Al-Anon. Support and self-help for the families and friends of alcoholics.

Alcoholics Anonymous. For people who are addicted to alcohol; provides support and help.

Local drug and alcohol agencies. Either independent community-based organizations or local branches of health and mental health departments.

Narcotics Anonymous. Often more receptive than Alcoholics Anonymous to adolescents who use drugs other than alcohol; provides support and help.

Parent support groups. Check with school counselors, local mental health departments, and other parents. Often these groups are informal and supported entirely by volunteer efforts.

A PROGRAM FOR YOUNG ADOLESCENTS AND THEIR FAMILIES

This book is part of *Skills for Adolescence,* a program developed jointly by Quest International and Lions Clubs International. The program offers a complete set of lessons for a semester course that helps to teach young adolescents skills they will need for healthy growth and positive decisions.

In addition to this book, the program provides a detailed, step-by-step teacher's manual for implementing the course, a student workbook, and a student notebook for personal reflections. The program includes intensive teacher training, parent involvement in many of the lessons and activities, and a series of meetings for parents on ways of coping with issues of early adolescence and improving family communication.

The seven units of the program focus on the following topics:

1. Entering the Teen Years: The Challenge Ahead
2. Building Self-confidence Through Better Communication
3. Learning About Emotions: Developing Competence in Self-assessment and Self-discipline
4. Friends: Improving Peer Relationships
5. Strengthening Family Relationships
6. Developing Critical-thinking Skills for Decision Making
7. Setting Goals for Healthy Living

Quest International is a nonprofit organization that specializes in programs for positive youth development. In addition to *Skills for Adolescence,* Quest has developed a wide range of programs focusing on positive youth development and highlighting parent and family involvement. Quest International is a founding member of the National Coalition for the Prevention of Drug and Alcohol Abuse.